PHILIP LARKIN

By BRUCE K. MARTIN

Drake University

TWAYNE PUBLISHERS

A DIVISION OF G. K. HALL & CO., BOSTON

For Barbara and Matt

Library of Congress Cataloging in Publication Data

Martin, Bruce, 1941-
Philip Larkin.

(Twayne's English authors series ; TEAS 234)
Bibliography: p. 155 - 62
Includes index.
1. Larkin, Philip—Criticism and interpretation.
PR6023.A66Z75   821'.'9'14   78-2696
ISBN 0-8057-6705-3

Contents

About the Author

Bruce K. Martin received his graduate training and degrees in English at the University of Cincinnati, and currently teaches at Drake University in Des Moines, Iowa, where he is an Associate Professor in the Department of English. His scholarly interests center on British literature of the nineteenth and twentieth centuries, as well as literary theory. He has published articles on George Eliot, Thackeray, Thomas Hardy, John Steinbeck, and Poe, and at present he is preparing a study of Hardy's poetry.

Preface

Since the mid-1950s Philip Larkin's reputation as a major figure in contemporary poetry has become increasingly secure. In writing this brief study of his works, I wish primarily to introduce American readers to the range and quality of his work. One of the striking things for me has been to discover how little known are the writings of this poet to most readers in the United States, in marked contrast with his prominence in England. Where one for some time often has been able to find paperback editions of all his collections and novels displayed in British bookstores, the paperback publication of *High Windows* in New York[1] represented the first American venture in this direction. Though his books are all in print and in demand in Britain, they are very hard to obtain in America, even in large stores. This is unfortunate, as Larkin's is a poetry which has much to say to American readers. The general unavailability of his poems to most Americans, except for a few selections in almost every major anthology, testifies to an American gap of awareness, which hopefully this study will help close.

As for readers already aware of Mr. Larkin's writing and stature, this book may introduce them to facets of his career of which they were previously unaware. While there have been several excellent essays on Larkin, only two books on him have appeared to date, by David Timms and Lolette Kuby respectively.[2] The differences between them illuminate another gap the present study attempts to close, for where Ms. Kuby admittedly avoids biographical and background discussion to concentrate as much as possible on the poems themselves, Timms examines Larkin's career largely from a social and biographical base, with much less of the concentrated and extended analysis Kuby offers. In this we have the split between American New Criticism and the traditional British "men of letters" approach. Because each approach has its merits, I have attempted to combine them, to examine both background and foreground for what they can tell us of Philip Larkin's writings. I have tried, too, to combine synthesis and analysis in examining his career, to see it as in many ways a single, broad development, yet made up of many discrete pieces which we call poems and which carry independent fascination and beauty.

I trust that the book's organization will reinforce this double view of Larkin. The first chapter traces his life by citing those events, forces, and people who seem to have influenced him most as an author. Next, in chapter two, comes a discussion of the poetic theory which Larkin has expressed and implied, and of The Movement in postwar British literature, to which he has been said to belong. Chapters three through five concentrate largely on his three major collections—*The Less Deceived, The Whitsun Weddings,* and *High Windows*—by examining first the peculiar world and world-view he establishes in his mature poetry, then the kinds of actions and effects generally shaping individual poems during this period, and finally the characteristic technical and stylistic tendencies helping produce the distinctly "Larkin" flavor in these poems. Chapter six considers in detail Larkin's prose writings—his novels and his essays on literature and jazz; while frequently cited earlier as background to the poetry, here they are analyzed and evaluated on their own terms. The next chapter concerns Larkin's overall development as a writer; here it becomes appropriate to offer extended discussion of his youthful collection, *The North Ship,* and to trace in detail its inadequacies and the directions in which he has moved during the thirty years since its first publication. The final chapter considers the various views toward his work expressed by critics, and his place in the larger English poetic tradition.

Because Larkin has published his collections more or less regularly, about every ten years since the mid-1940s, and because we know that he publishes individual poems with an equal regularity, perhaps four or five each year, it is both necessary and misleading to speak of particular poems as parts of collections. Each of his mature collections seems to blend into the next. For this reason I have in my central chapters treated the poems of his maturity as separate parts of one whole, rather than three, and have regarded his development as more gradual and imperceptible than grouping them by collection might suggest. However, because each of the collections does possess distinctive qualities and does represent a milestone in Larkin's career, an awareness of where particular poems fit into the chronology of that career is surely helpful. To facilitate such awareness, I have included under the bibliographical entry for each of the main collections a list of the poems which it contains.

Acknowledgments

Many institutions and people have helped me in many ways as I have written this study. I must acknowledge the leave granted me by Drake University for the Spring 1974 term, which permitted me to travel to England and gather some of the materials for this study. Relatedly I must thank the Drake Research Council for a generous travel grant and for additional support in obtaining and duplicating relevant material. While in London I benefited from the courtesies of the British Museum and the University of London library. In particular I should mention the kindness of Dr. Anthea Baird of the University of London's Music Library, and the bibliographical help generously extended me since my return to the United States by Mr. B. C. Bloomfield of the University of London's Oriental and African Studies library. At Drake, besides being encouraged by the frequent advice of colleagues, I have been aided, often daily, by members of the Cowles Library staff, particularly by the Reference Department. Finally and foremost I am pleased to record my thanks to my wife, Barbara, whose patience, support, and several readings of the manuscript have helped greatly.

Acknowledgments are due to Faber and Faber for permission to quote from *The North Ship, The Whitsun Weddings, Jill, A Girl in Winter,* and *All What Jazz;* to the Marvell Press for permission to quote from *The Less Deceived;* to Farrar, Straus & Giroux for permission to quote from *High Windows;* and to Philip Larkin himself for kindly permitting me to quote from his uncollected poems.

Chronology

1922   August 9, Philip Arthur Larkin born at Coventry, Warwickshire.

1930   Attends King Henry VIII School, Conventry.

1940

1940   "Ultimatum" published in the *Listener.* September, matriculates to St. John's College, Oxford.

1943   B.A., with first-class honors in English. Appointed librarian at the public library in Wellington, Shropshire.

1944   Several poems published in *Poetry from Oxford in Wartime,* edited by William Bell.

1945   *The North Ship* published by The Fortune Press.

1946   Appointed assistant librarian at University College, Leicester. *Jill* published by Faber and Faber.

1947   M.A., Oxford. *A Girl in Winter* published by Faber and Faber.

1950   Appointed sublibrarian at Queen's University, Belfast. Publishes *XX Poems* at his own expense.

1953   Some of his poems published by Peter Owen in *Springtime.*

1954   Some of his poems published in a Fantasy pamphlet.

1955   Appointed librarian of the Brynmor Jones Library, University of Hull. *The Less Deceived* published by the Marvell Press.

1961   Begins reviewing jazz and jazz recordings for the *Daily Telegraph.*

1964   *The Whitsun Weddings* published by Faber and Faber. Revised edition of *Jill,* with Larkin's own introduction, published by Faber and Faber.

1965   Awarded the Queen's Gold Medal for Poetry and the Arts Council Triennial Award for Poetry.

1966   Revised edition of *The North Ship,* with his own introduction, published by Faber and Faber.

1969   Awarded honorary D. Lit. degree by Queen's University, Belfast.

1970   *All What Jazz* published by Macmillan.
1970   Visiting Fellow of All Souls College, Oxford.
1971
1973   *The Oxford Book of Twentieth-Century English Verse*, chosen by Philip Larkin, published by Oxford.
1974   *High Windows* published by Faber and Faber.

CHAPTER 1

Life and Career

PHILIP Larkin is both difficult and easy for biographical treatment in a study such as this. His poetry suggests a marked identity between speaker and poet; frequently his poems seem highly personal, and the personality seeming so near the poem's surface arouses the reader's liking, interest, and curiosity. Having repeatedly eschewed the modernist notion of masking and impersonality in his own writing and having deplored its excesses in the work of others, Larkin projects a sincerity and forthrightness by which he unwittingly invites speculation and investigation about himself.

Where Yeats and Eliot attempted to hide behind the deliberately contrived personae of their poems and thus teased readers, critics, and scholars into exploring the men behind the masks, Larkin, by baring himself in his poems and by appearing a twentieth-century "man speaking to men," ironically has raised in the minds of many readers questions which his poems cannot, and which he will not, answer. And, while his frequently expressed doubt that the poet deserves more study than other men, his insistence that he certainly does not merit such examination, and his refusal to become a public personality, suggest a perhaps admirable modesty and a certainly understandable desire for privacy, they serve also to tantalize the reader or critic bent on a heroic or biographical view of the poet. Such a bent Larkin has satirized in a recent poem, "Posterity," where he imagines his literary biographer, an American academician forced to "do" him in a dissertation, bemoaning the ordinariness of his subject: "Not out of kicks or something happening— / One of those old-type *natural* fouled-up guys."

The seeming ease of recounting Philip Larkin's life suggests that he may be right about himself and writers in general. Certainly the available facts support such a view. Born in 1922 in Coventry, a manufacturing city one hundred miles northwest of London, he

13

grew up in modest circumstances; his father served as city treasurer from 1922 to 1944. Characteristically Larkin has written off his childhood as something he cannot much remember, and as probably not much worth remembering. Many readers have taken as a definitive statement on this matter the amusing disclaimer in "I Remember, I Remember," where he wittily excludes all of the stock romantic excitement from his childhood.

However, if nothing very extraordinary happened in his childhood, the ordinary things he can remember suggest both distinctive and characteristic lines of development. A lively imagination is revealed by the series of complicated cricket games, using cards and dice, which he managed to maintain for several years.[1] And, among his many childhood friends and playmates he has recalled a boy named Arthur, in whose imaginary rugby games, cinema schedules, and orchestra the young Larkin first recognized "the power to create and sustain private worlds."[2] Because during these years he was an avid reader of detective novels, his poem "A Study of Reading Habits" may well describe his own fantasizing in the hero's role—"It was worth ruining my eyes / To know I could still keep cool, / And deal out the old right hook / To dirty dogs twice my size"—which in adolescence became identification with the villain: "Later, with inch-thick specs, / Evil was just my lark."

All of this might seem very ordinary play of the imagination were it not accompanied by a growing interest in serious reading and in serious writing. Larkin himself has cited his father's liking for books as the only really significant fact of his youth. The books which he was thus able to read included not only the standard fare of the respectable family library, but some authors and works more advanced for the time. As he has said: "Not till I was much older did I realize that most boys of my class were brought up to regard Galsworthy and Chesterton as the apex of modern literature, and to think Somerset Maugham a bit 'hot.' I was therefore lucky."[3] His wide reading at home of such writers as Hardy, Wilde, Butler, Shaw, Lawrence, Aldous Huxley, and Katherine Mansfield he supplemented by frequent trips to the local library, where he borrowed books in great quantity.

He matched such voracious reading with almost equally voracious writing. Sometime in his mid-teens he began routinely to write verse and prose each night. Though describing these juvenile writings as self-indulgence spurred by puberty and viewing most of them as "excruciating" attempts at humor, he has regretted the absence of similar industry in his adult years. Of the few things he published in the school magazine, most were either romantic lyric poems or prose dramatic monologues. The former, which have been described as "typically adolescent,"[4] obviously led to the kind of writing contained in his first published collection, *The North Ship*, while the latter, dealing mostly with the comic frustration of inept central characters, represent a bent transferred to verse in the best-known of his later poems. Most of his schoolboy writing, though, went unpublished.

Besides a lively imagination and a zest for reading and writing, Larkin early developed a third interest which has strongly colored his personal and literary development, his interest in jazz. He has spoken of this youthful enthusiasm and has surmised that the emotional impact of the great jazz artists approximated that of the great romantic poets on sensitive youth a century earlier.[5] He has further confessed that jazz has meant more to him than poetry; adapting Baudelaire, he admits, "You might say that I can live a week without poetry but not a day without jazz."[6] This fierce love for jazz may have begun as a means of youthful escape from the pressures of school. Certainly it involved listening to 78 RPM records at local shops and on home record players, scrupulously buying and swapping new cuts by top jazz artists, and catching visiting performers and bands—all of which Larkin has termed the "golden hours" of his youth in the 1930s. "Oh, play that thing! . . . / On me your voice falls as they say love should, / Like an enormous yes," he has written of the great saxophonist Sidney Bechet, one of his special favorites. While the meaning of jazz to Larkin is very personal, it seems safe to say that this kind of music has helped keep him and his poetry from the conventional directions his background might otherwise have dictated, and has thus contributed to the character he so insistently denies.

Certainly jazz linked his youth with the next stage of his life, Oxford, and perhaps eased the difficulties of going off to college during wartime. His matriculation to St. John's College in the fall of 1940 reflected more his and his parents' concern for his getting in a year at Oxford before going to war than his academic achievements, for during his ten years at King Henry VIII school in Coventry he had been, for the most part, a mediocre student. He seems to have regarded school as a tiresome interruption to things he liked to do much better and has admitted, "I was very stupid until I could concentrate on English."[7] Oxford, where he could pursue such a specialty, proved much more pleasant and academically rewarding. His expectations of conscription went unconfirmed as he eventually failed his military physical exam and was able to stay at Oxford until taking a first-class honors degree in 1943.

Wartime Oxford differed markedly from peacetime Oxford. Austerity measures such as rationing and blackouts were in effect. The draft had taken many of the older men who normally would constitute the bulk of the student body, while most of the undergraduates who were Larkin's contemporaries expected to be drafted after a year or two. Thus there was in some ways a more serious atmosphere than might otherwise mark the university scene. One of the interesting aspects of *Jill*, his first novel, is the record of wartime Oxford which it presents. John Kemp, the inept protagonist, reflects the doubts coloring the attempts of his college mates to maintain the high-jinks atmosphere traditional among undergraduates. Besides noting the peculiar regulations brought on by the war, the novel depicts student uncertainty about staying at Oxford very long, their concern for families as London and other British towns were being bombed, and a general alternation between wanting to attend to the frivolous and wanting to seize the substantial in the face of a very uncertain future. In Kemp and many others like him we see young men forced to decisions about themselves and their values long before society would ordinarily demand such decisions. Although serving mostly as a backdrop to Kemp's personal difficulties, the war contributes to the complexity of those difficulties. In this Kemp seems typical of his generation.

For many people such changes at Oxford during the war signified a loss. Larkin, however, regards himself as fortunate to have been there during wartime. He has noted the almost complete suspension of concern for mere employment: "There were none of the pressing dilemmas of teaching or Civil Service, industry or America, publishing or journalism: in consequence, there was next to no careerism. National affairs were going so badly, and a victorious peace was clearly so far off, that effort expended on one's post-war prospects could hardly seem anything but a ludicrous waste of time."[8] He feels that the lack of gentility in the student body during the war was certainly balanced by the lack of foolishness, and that students benefited from a truer perspective on life that a peacetime college experience might have given them: "At an age when self-importance would have been normal, events cut us ruthlessly down to size."[9]

One of the more peculiar aspects of the Oxford situation at this time was the constant arriving and departing of students. "Friends remained plentiful, but contemporaries were becoming scarce," Larkin has observed.[10] Of his several warm and lasting friendships at Oxford, probably the most important and best known is that with Kingsley Amis, a friendship reflected implicitly in numerous writings by each, and explicitly in the dedication of Amis's first novel, *Lucky Jim,* "to Philip Larkin," in Larkin's dedication of *XX Poems* to Amis, and in his writing "Born Yesterday" for Amis's daughter Sally. While Larkin has been mentioned as the model for Jim Dixon, the hero of Amis's comic novel, Larkin's fond recollections of Amis's brilliant talent for amusing imitations and pranks suggest that the character of Lucky Jim was at least partly self-inspired. Indeed, Larkin has said of Amis's knack for mimicry, "[F]or the first time I felt myself in the presence of a talent greater than my own"[11]—a remark suggesting a greater degree of self-assurance in the young Larkin than might otherwise be assumed. Further, he has claimed that whatever humor he has been able to put into his poetry has been the result of trying to imagine what Amis, with his exacting standard of wit, would find amusing.

Besides laughing at Amis's jokes and imitations, the circle of undergraduates with whom Larkin associated at Oxford spent a great deal of time talking, listening to jazz, and drinking. Though interested in literature, they were decidedly, and perhaps somewhat self-consciously, unacademic in their approach to literary matters. Though a talented group of poets had blossomed at Oxford during the early years of the war, the Amis-Larkin circle would have nothing to do with them, apparently regarding them as culturally too narrow and snobbish.

Oxford and the period of time spent there unquestionably and understandably have meant much to Larkin. His scorn of literary biography or autobiography attending too much to childhood or youth—his claim that his own biography might well begin when he was twenty-one[12]—indicates how significant Oxford was for him as an ending and a beginning. Certainly it represents the first of those focal points of comparison which characters in his poems frequently employ in examining the quality of their lives. For example, the speaker in "Dockery and Son," born in 1922, goes back to his old college and meditates on the difference in direction he and a classmate have taken. Like *Jill,* the poem suggests the kinds of experiences Larkin had at Oxford as it refers to undergraduate drinking and related antics, but, written almost twenty years after *Jill*, it suggests, too, the continuing sharpness of such experience in his memory.

If friends and fun contributed importantly to his undergraduate life, studies and writing were not neglected. During his first years at Oxford Larkin expected to be drafted; not until after four terms did he fail the physical exam. In anticipation of the draft he had burned his notes and therefore had to work feverishly to prepare for examinations. Since he ultimately graduated with first-class honors, he has recalled with relish his tutor's report that "Mr. Larkin has taken his schools and if the papers suit him he may get a second and if they do not he will have to be content with a third."[13]

As for writing, the demands and distractions of undergraduate life caused a slowdown from the productive pace he had set back in Coventry. Immediately before arriving at Oxford, in the summer of 1940, he had sent four poems to the *Listener*, which accepted one, entitled "Ultimatum," having to do with the war and Britain's role in it. This was his first poem published other than in the Coventry school paper. At Oxford he continued to write poems; some were published in undergraduate magazines, and some eventually appeared in the anthology *Poetry in Wartime from Oxford*, which also contained the work of several other poets, including W. J. Harvey, Christopher Middleton, and Roy Porter.

Two friends made late in his Oxford period especially influenced his writing. One was Bruce Montgomery, known to lovers of detective fiction as "Edmund Crispin." Larkin did not meet Montgomery until his final term, but has noted how Montgomery's "modern languages - playhouse, classical music - Randolph Hotel ambience" conflicted with his own bent and that of most of his friends. The two became drinking partners, however, and widened each other's awareness: Larkin introduced Montgomery to many jazz artists, while Montgomery shared his "intellectual epicureanism."[14] The three years of his closest friendship with Montgomery represented a peak period of creativity for Larkin. The dedication of *A Girl in Winter* suggests his gratitude to Montgomery as a catalyst for such productivity.

The particular form of his poetry was influenced by another friend made late in his Oxford career, Vernon Watkins. Watkins, a close friend of Dylan Thomas and himself a poet of distinction, visited the English Club at Oxford, where Larkin heard him read and discuss poetry. They became friends, corresponded while

Watkins was away in the air force, and discussed the poems Larkin was writing. Larkin has said of his first collection, *The North Ship*, " 'F / Sgt. Watkins, V' was the book's kindest and almost only critic."[15] Specifically, Watkins steered Larkin onto Yeats; the quality of almost all the poems in *The North Ship* reflects Larkin's trying to reproduce the kind of poetic voice pointed out to him by Watkins. Though he ultimately rejected that voice in favor of one he regarded as more genuinely his, Watkins's encouragement and friendly criticism at this time stimulated the younger poet to write and to consider more closely the kind of poetry he wished to write.

The stimulus of friends like Montgomery and Watkins, plus the freedom from academic obligations upon his leaving Oxford in 1943, resulted in the most productive period of Larkin's career. After *Poetry from Oxford in Wartime* came out with some of his poems, in October 1944 he received a letter from the Fortune Press asking for a collection. He quickly sent in thirty poems, which appeared as *The North Ship* in July 1945. These poems, with few exceptions, reflect Larkin's preoccupation with the poetic models acquired from Watkins. Indeed, he recounts how after supper each evening, before writing, he would "limber up" by looking through his copy of Yeats.[16]

At the close of his time at Oxford, Larkin faced the question of a career which the war had permitted him to postpone. His decision to become a librarian, which he has been ever since, represents more chance than vocation. Uncertain what to do, but forced by pressure from the Ministry of Labour to seek some serious work, he accepted his first offer, the librarian's post at the public library in the small Shropshire town of Wellington.[17] After a few years there, he moved to University College, Leicester, serving as assistant librarian, and then, in 1950, to Belfast as sublibrarian at Queen's University. Since 1955 he has served as head librarian at the University of Hull, located in an industrial and fishing center 150 miles north of London.

Larkin's attitude toward his work and toward work in general is amusingly ambivalent. Characteristically he has noted how largely by chance the pattern of his adult life was determined. As for the work itself, he claims to like the way librarianship combines administration and academia, and has admitted that it gives him experiences and material for poetry which a fulltime career of writing might not afford. On the other hand, he has occasionally regretted that his work is not his art; while feeling he probably writes better without the undisciplined idleness of a writer's life, he sometimes wishes he could be certain by experiencing such idleness.[18]

This vacillation between attraction and repulsion toward work comes out in two of his better-known poems, "Toads" and "Toads Revisited." In the first he begins questioning why he allows work to "squat" on his life, then gradually decides that "something sufficiently toadlike" squats in him, too, the result being an impasse between envy and scorn for those able to avoid the work routine, which he suspects to be rationalization for his own cowardice. In the sequel he ignores the moral implications of work and idleness to concentrate on the satisfaction gained through each, concluding with exaggerated surrender, "Give me your arm, old toad; / Help me down Cemetery Road." If not entirely satisfactory, work seems an improvement over idleness, especially in middle age. This half-amusement at his own ambivalence toward his work comes out, too, in his speaking of his position at Hull as "that nice little Shetland pony of a job you so confidently bestride in the beginning [which] suddenly grows to a frightful Grand National Winner."[19] Though such winning has its merits, so do other pursuits.

Initially at least, Larkin's life as a librarian contributed to his writing. His productive outburst during the years at Wellington reflects the routine conducive to writing which he established there. Writing every evening from nine to midnight, he was able to work out the bulk of the poems contained in *The North Ship*, to complete *Jill*, and to write another novel, *A Girl in Winter*, which drew heavily on his Wellington experience. Though neither the publication of *Jill* in 1946 nor *A Girl in Winter* a year later stirred up much critical response, they inspired Larkin to try writing more fiction. In fact, he has described the period from 1945 to 1950 as "one long, dreary attempt to write a third novel."[20] Late in this period he realized that his impulse to write fiction could only lead him to a dead end, and that he could better express himself in poems.

Unfortunately, his abortive attempts at the third novel were accompanied by equally frustrating attempts to find and write a kind of poetry which satisfied him. He had turned to fiction because of his feeling that he could not go further with his poetry as it had developed. Compared with the poems he had written at Oxford, his two novels exhibited a much more concrete tone and style, as well as a considerably greater degree of humor. In his introduction to the 1966 edition of *The North Ship*, Larkin has recounted his growing dissatisfaction with what he elsewhere has termed the style of "the surrealists and the New Apocalypse crowd."[21] He credits the discovery, or the rediscovery, of Thomas Hardy's poems, while he was at Wellington, with his eventual escape from the uneasy hold Yeats had on him. While the shift from the kind of poems in *The North Ship* to that of his later collections was gradual, his shift of allegiance was rather quick. But, because confusion over poetic styles was compounded by his continuing desire to specialize in fiction, not until the late 1940s did he totally, and finally, abandon his earlier, Yeatsian style in his verse. John Kemp of *Jill* can be seen as a youthful prototype of the speakers in many of Larkin's later poems, while *A Girl in Winter* likewise fastens on many of the concerns informing his later poetry. His repeated starts at the third novel presumably represent attempts at doing the kind of thing he eventually did in his best-known poems. Not until abandoning fiction entirely was he able to combine the subject matter of his novels with a comfortable poetic technique.

The move to Belfast in 1950 encouraged such a combination and ended the fallow period in Larkin's writing career. Finding the city and university stimulating, he managed during his five years there to write many of the poems contained in *The Less Deceived*, including several of his most famous. Where Oxford and Wellington were directly reflected in his writings, only a couple of poems, "Church Going" and "The Importance of Elsewhere" (later published in *The Whitsun Weddings*), refer directly to his stay in Ireland. In this later poem he underscores a central reason he was able to write so much and so well while in Belfast, for he remarks that where in Ireland "The salt rebuff of speech, / Insisting so on difference, made me welcome: / Once that was recognized, we were in touch"—in England he did not have the luxury of being "Separate": "Here no elsewhere underwrites my existence." It has been suggested, too, that the presence of Donald Davie at Trinity College, Dublin, and the appointment of Anthony Hartley as literary editor of *The Spectator* during this time proved not insignificant factors in freeing Larkin from his earlier frustrations, as both men encouraged the kind of poetry later associated with The Movement.

Though writing many of his finest poems in Belfast, he failed to publish them in collection or to win critical recognition while there. Aside from single poems in magazines, usually *The Spectator*, his publication during this period was limited to a privately printed pamphlet titled *XX Poems*, five poems in the anthology *Springtime*

(1953), and five others in a Fantasy pamphlet (1954). The first of these, brought out in 1951, he tried to distribute to leading critics and literary figures. It went mostly ignored, though, partly because—in a move worthy of the self-defeating speakers of many of his poems—he sent copies out with penny stamps just after the postage had been raised to 1½ pence.

Publication of *The Less Deceived* and consequent acclaim came to Larkin only after he had tried unsuccessfully to interest a Dublin publisher in it, and after he had left Belfast for the post at Hull. George Hartley, a young poetry enthusiast and owner of the fledgling Marvell Press in Yorkshire, had admired Larkin's poems and had written him in Belfast asking for a collection. Larkin happily obliged and arrived in Hull at about the time Hartley had finished the printing and binding of the collection. After Larkin, partly from Hartley's insistence, changed the title from *Various Poems* to *The Less Deceived*, distribution began in late 1955.

The book's reception was phenomenal. Where *XX Poems* had been acknowledged by only a few of the many people to whom Larkin sent copies, *The Less Deceived* gained prompt notice in the *Times* and favorable comment in other reviews, its subscription issue was quickly sold out and additional printings ordered, and in 1958 another edition was issued and the book imported to the United States. It has thus far gone into six editions, while its no less acclaimed successor, *The Whitsun Weddings* (1964), went into its fifth impression in 1970.

The unexpected success of *The Less Deceived* quickly established Philip Larkin's reputation as one of Britain's leading poets. Many recognitions—the Queen's Gold Medal, the Arts Council Award, an honorary doctorate from Queen's University, Belfast, and a fellowship at All Souls, Oxford—followed, as well as numerous requests for readings, lectures, and interviews, which, with characteristic modesty, he has tended to refuse.

After rather rapid emergence as a major poet Larkin branched out into other areas of publishing. In the late 1950s he began writing reviews and review-articles, mostly on contemporary poets and on new collections of older poets. He emerged as an anthologist, first in collaboration (*New Poems*, with Louis MacNiece and Bonamy Dobree, 1958) and then by himself in *The Oxford Book of Twentieth-Century English Verse*, published in 1973. His being selected to edit the distinguished Oxford collection suggests the esteem in which he is held in the literary world.

Another new area of writing—and for him the most pleasant—is the jazz reviewing he has done for the *Daily Telegraph* since 1961; he has turned out a series of witty reviews on new recordings and re-releases of older ones.

Larkin's life now revolves around his work as a librarian, his writing, and his continuing interest in jazz. He confines himself mostly to Hull, and never goes abroad. "As I get older," he says, "I grow increasingly impatient of holidays: they seem a wholly feminine conception, based on an impotent dislike of everyday life and a romantic notion that it will all be better at Frinton or Venice."[22] Continuing to limit himself to an average of four or five published poems each year—though more are begun and never completed or never released—he has most recently published *High Windows*, his long-awaited fourth collection. Characteristically he refuses to predict drastic changes in his life or in his writing, though he admits wanting to try different kinds of poems from those usually associated with him.

CHAPTER 2

The Larkin Poetic

TO speak of a "Larkin poetic" is, on the surface at least, a contradiction in terms, since Larkin has shown extreme reluctance to comment broadly on the nature of poetry or the obligations of the poet. While such wariness, and the nonheroic view of the poet which it implies, reflect in part his modesty, they reflect also his firm conviction that broad theorizing by a poet, or preoccupation with the theories of others, may inhibit his writing in his best or most characteristic fashion. "It is fatal to decide, intellectually, what good poetry is because you are then in honour bound to try to write it, instead of the poems that only you can write," he has explained.[1] He has further insisted that not only does he find "abstracted views" on poetry no help in writing, but that he must pointedly avoid reaching such views. Thus he notes his sense of relief upon discovering Hardy's poetry: "I didn't have to try and jack myself up to a concept of poetry that lay outside my own style."[2] Even while admitting his own preferences among other poets and delineating the kind of poetry he attempts to create, Larkin wishes no rules prohibiting the range of poetry, since for him each poet creates his own unique poetic.

I *Larkin on Art*

Despite his disinclination to assume the role of a theoretician, Larkin's poetry is sufficiently distinguishable and definable to warrant the assignment of some fairly definite commitments to him as a poet—in alliance with some poets, and in opposition to others. More important, the relatively small body of his published comment about poetry clarifies explicitly the view of poetry only implied in his poems. Also useful in this regard are the remarks about art in his jazz reviews, for where he tries to avoid theorizing in his role as a poet, his post as discriminating listener and public critic of

24

jazz forces him to theorize. His wholehearted acceptance of this obligation has resulted not only in pleasant and provocative discussions of jazz, but in an important addition to his sparse commentary on poetry.

For example, his most sustained aversion in art is toward modernism, an aversion expressed most openly in his introduction to *All What Jazz*, the collection of his jazz reviews. There he amusingly describes his shock upon being exposed to postwar jazz, as opposed to the traditional variety he had loved since childhood. Having been separated from jazz during the final years of the war and the years immediately afterwards, and having been reunited with a record player in the late 1940s, he found the "new" jazz developing with the advent of the long-playing record not only unpleasant, but mysteriously unpleasant, until he recognized the connection between modern jazz and modernism in the other arts.

At the center of modernism in jazz, in literature, and in the visual arts, Larkin sees the artist's excessive concern with technical experimentation. Grouping the American saxophonist Charlie Parker with Ezra Pound and Picasso as representative exponents of modernism, he complains of their "irresponsible exploitation of technique in contradiction of human life as we know it."[3] Technique calling attention to itself takes the form in Parker of wildly innovative solos which, for Larkin, lead nowhere except away from the recognizable. Noting the features of "wild, bubbling freedom" characteristic of Parker's playing, he asks, "But freedom from what?": "As one listens to Parker spiralling away 'out of this world,' as the phrase goes, one can only answer 'humanity,' and that is a fatal thing for an artist, or an art, to be separated from."[4]

Such alienation Larkin sees as one of the principal components of modernism in every art: "Piqued at being neglected, the [artist] has painted portraits with both eyes on the same side of the nose, or smothered a model with paint and rolled her over a blank canvas. He has designed a dwelling-house to be built underground. He has written poems resembling the kind of pictures typists make with their machines during coffee breaks, or a novel in gibberish, or a play in which the characters sit in dustbins."[5] The blatant technique of modern art is contrasted, too, with the order produced by form in more traditional art, an order evident in Larkin's poems. Such form may not be traditional and should not be imposed; rather, it should be appropriate to the subject and feeling developed. But, because Larkin insists that art relate recognizably to "this world" of human experience and feeling, technique should operate as the means for capturing and defining such experience for the listener, viewer, or reader.

Besides the modernist tendency away from recognizably real experience, Larkin deplores the tendency toward irresponsibility in modern art. Specifically he scorns art which neglects its audience or which demands undue academicism for understanding it. Such, he feels, has been the case with too much modern literature: "The terms and the arguments vary with circumstances, but basically the message is: 'Don't trust your eyes, or ears, or understanding. They'll tell you this is ridiculous, or ugly, or meaningless. Don't believe them. You've got to work at this: after all, you don't expect to understand anything as important as art straight off, do you? I mean, this is pretty complex stuff: if you want to know how complex, I'm giving a course of 96 lectures at the local college, starting next week.' "[6] And he has insisted as a "guiding principle" that a poem, and presumably any work of art, ought not to require as a *sine qua non* of its explication an awareness of tradition; rather, it ought to create its own world. In fact, he feels that the better the poem the less likely it is to call attention to the period in which it is written: "If I were shown a work 'today' that could be placed only somewhere within the last fifty years, I should wonder if I were not in the presence of a considerable talent."[7]

Larkin's distrust of the academic in poetry suggests his desire for a wider circle of readers than most modernist poets have reached. He feels that most of the responsibility for the growing rift between poetry and the general public in the twentieth century rests with the poets. Rejecting as elitist and antihumanist the modernist demands that readers must be better educated, Larkin feels that poetry must return to the people, that it must win the reader back from his pub and television. He therefore admires a poet like John Betjeman, who can embrace the public and be embraced by them. He admires Betjeman and any other poet who appeals sincerely to the common emotional denominator of his readers, and deplores contemporary poets who minimize such common humanity. Such poets, he feels, have produced a "new kind of bad poetry": "not the old kind that tries to move the reader and fails, but one that does not even try."[8] He endorses Betjeman's premodernist belief in poetry as an essentially emotional business, his honesty in conveying emotion, and his evident acceptance of his readers, even their weaknesses. "Energy most modern poets spend on screening their impulses for security Betjeman puts into the poems," Larkin claims.[9]

For Larkin poetry is mostly a matter of communication and of the poet's accommodating his readers as presumably literate but not esoterically schooled. He defines poetry as "emotional in nature and theatrical in operation, a skilled re-creation of emotion in other people."[10] This emphasis on the rhetorical and the commonplace causes Larkin to complain that today the audience is being forgotten and that a "cunning merger" between poet, literary critic, and academic critic has replaced the old, pleasure-seeking audience of poetry with a "humbler squad" seeking self-improvement, "an essentially student audience, believing they must match the mental equipment of the poet."[11] The imbalance between the humility of such readers and egocentricity of such poets must be corrected, lest the gap between poetry and life widen so much that the poet is totally isolated and poetry no longer viewed as an art.

Frightened by such a prospect, Larkin urges reader and poet to realize its dangers. Readers should be more honest about what pleases and what bores them. They should demand that a poem give them something besides a sense of inadequacy in dealing with it. If a poem presents a puzzle, it should seem a puzzle worth solving by virtue of the poem's unpuzzling emotional appeal, and not a pointless academic game. The poet must learn to regard himself as a person, and in a Wordsworthian sense, as a person speaking to persons. This is what Larkin himself discovered in the late 1940s when he altered his approach to writing poetry. Never having felt quite comfortable with the various notions of poetry derived from others, he finally realized that he could depend on his own feelings for the appropriate manner in which to present such material. He learned from Thomas Hardy that his own life, with its often casual discoveries, could become poems, and that he could legitimately share such experience with his readers. From this lesson has come his belief that a poem is better based on something from "unsorted" experience than on another poem or other art.

The technical key to such poetry is, of course, clarity, while its bane is obscurity. Larkin has said that he writes poems to preserve some of his experiences for others and to keep them from oblivion: "Some years ago I came to the conclusion that to write a poem was to construct a verbal device that would preserve an experience indefinitely by reproducing it in whoever read the poem."[12] This preservation, which Anthony Thwaite terms "verbal pickling," requires not only a keen awareness of the experience itself and a variety of literary skills, but a sense of how best to transfer such awareness to the reader through such skills.

Having seen how Larkin deplores pointless or conspicuous technique, we can understand not only many of his practices as a poet, but his special admiration for writers like Hardy, Edward Thomas, the early W. H. Auden, and Betjeman, in whom technique is notably inconspicuous, and his reservations less about the giants among modernist poets than their more recent followers. Where he praises Betjeman for using meter and rhyme as means of enhancing the emotion of a poem and for trying to communicate meaning directly, rather than symbolically,[13] he complains of the "tortured syntax, pointless mystification, [and] lack of humor" in a book by one of Betjeman's contemporaries.[14] Larkin's emphasis here, as usual, is on the poet's obligation to his reader: to move and please, perhaps to amuse, but never to ignore.

II   Larkin and The Movement

Larkin's views on art and literature match very closely the general attitudes attributed to a group of writers with which he has been associated, known as The Movement. While critics have debated whether Larkin's poetry is, in fact, "Movement" poetry, and while we can better determine that after examining his poems, there can be no question that his basic stance on the problems of modern poetry, the relationship of the poet to the reading public, and certain directions which British poetry ought to take, suggest a close alliance with the other so-called Movement writers.

The difficulty of determining his relationship to The Movement stems partly from the fact that the authors usually named in this connection never banded together, even informally, as any sort of literary school in the conventional sense. The Movement label, however useful for reference, is at best the invention of critics applied after the fact to a group of writers in many ways similar yet in many ways sufficiently dissimilar and sufficiently distrustful of the label to require one to use it cautiously. The term "Movement" surfaced in an anonymous article published in the *Spectator* in late 1954[15] noting certain shared tendencies among younger writers who had emerged in the early 1950s. The names mentioned by the reviewer were Donald Davie, Thom Gunn, John Wain, Kinglsey Amis, and Iris Murdoch. As the article preceded the publication of

The Less Deceived, Larkin's name— almost always mentioned in this connection once his reputation was established—was absent. The Movement writers—and to the *Spectator* list were, eventually added the names of John Holloway, Elizabeth Jennings, and D. J. Enright, as well as Larkin's, while that of Miss Murdoch was removed—are generally characterized more by what they oppose than what they favor. As Robert Conquest, whose anthology *New Lines* included all of the Movement poets and whose introduction to that collection constituted something of a manifesto of Movement poetry (not necessarily subscribed to by any of the contributors), has remarked, there is not so much a common doctrine among these authors as the determination to avoid bad principles.[16] Foremost among such bad principles are the various experimental techniques associated with Modernism, as well as the largely exclusive view of poetry and poets which modernism tended to foster. All of these writers have called, implicitly in their poetry and fiction and explicitly in critical essays, for some sort of commonsense return to more traditional techniques. The rationale for this antimodernist, antiexperimental stance is their stated concern with clarity: with writing distinguished by precision rather than obscurity. Relatedly the Movement writers reacted against the excess of emotional fervor and wounded sensibility they saw in much poetry of the 1930s and 1940s, and urged instead not an abandonment of emotion, but a mixture of rationality with feeling, of objective control with subjective abandon. Their notion of what they felt the earlier generation of writers, particularly poets, lacked, centered around the ideas of honesty and realism about self and about the outside world. As Conquest says of Movement poetry: "It submits to no great system of theoretical construction nor agglomeration of unconscious commands. It is free from both mystical and logical compulsions and —like modern philosophy—is empirical in its attitude toward all that comes. This reverence for the real person or event is, indeed, a part of the general intellectual ambience (in so far as that is not blind or retrogressive) of our time."[17]

Critics have linked this empiricist tendency with such things as the disillusionment following the holocaust of World War II and the linguistic positivism of Wittgenstein and his followers popular at Oxford, where most of the Movement writers studied.[18] Leslie Fiedler sees them joined together in such things as their skepticism toward the classless ideals of the Welfare State, their "post-post Christian" boredom with the religious concerns of the Bloomsbury group, their sense of the implied reader of their poetry as a Common Reader, and their emphasis upon the realistic details of drab modern England.[19]

Certainly they all represent broadly similar social and educational backgrounds. Certainly, too, they embrace a reading public extending beyond the limits of that background. Whether such things explain the Movement or justify such a label is difficult to tell. From their work which gave rise to the label—in various Fantasy Press books and pamphlets, the anthology *Springtime*, and Conquest's *New Lines*—the Movement poets have developed in different directions, as if The Movement began to disintegrate as soon as it had been formulated in the minds of critics. Whether the countermovement known as The Group and Dennis Enright's collection, *Poets of the 1950's* (1955), represented reactions against these writers for what they actually were, or for what they were said to be, is not easy to say.

Certainly, though, there was a limited cohesion of attitude toward literature and its relation to life among the Movement writers. And, the Movement position approximated in general spirit, if not always in particular detail, the poetic of Philip Larkin. In this sense Larkin deserves to be considered a part, and an important part, of The Movement.

CHAPTER 3

The Larkin World

L ARKIN'S reputation as a leading contemporary poet
rests mainly on *The Less Deceived* and *The Whitsun Weddings.*
His earlier poetry and his prose writings are generally regarded as
interesting backdrops to the richer and more characteristic work in
those two collections of verse. And, though *High Windows* may
signal a departure from those poems published in the 1950s and early 1960s, it probably will not alter the image of Larkin derived from
them. While Larkin's repeatedly expressed wish to write different
kinds of poems may reflect his discomfort with that image, whether
the kind of poetry it suggests is as limited as some have maintained
or whether he has escaped the pattern assigned to him are questions
better answered after a careful examination of his poetic development. Clearly the kind of poems associated most often with Larkin
reflect these two very popular collections.

One reason for the popularity of his poems is the apparent com-
monplaceness of their subjects. Larkin manages to project a very
personal concern for the things which personally concern most people living in the modern world. This is why one critic has credited
him with combining a "sharp contemporary relevance" with universality, to appeal to readers' sense not only of what life in general
is about, but what the individual's life today is about,[1] while
another has applauded his willingness to "[traffic] in the truth of ordinary life."[2] The world of his poems is a world to which most
readers can readily respond.

I   Time and Place

For one thing, the Larkin world is a recognizably postwar British
world. Unlike many recent poets, and even some with whom he is
often associated as a technician, Larkin chooses to specify a
demonstrably British and demonstrably contemporary background

31

for his poems. His settings are usually those of the large town or city) heavily trafficked streets, urban parks filled with mothers and playing children, the hospital in the midst of a business district, the discotheque, the tawdry rooming house, the pet shop, and even the interiors of the semidetached houses making up much of British suburbia.

While the degree of specificity varies from poem to poem, Larkin does not hesitate on occasion to include those gritty details suggestive of life for most Britons today. His poems casually note "crowds, colourless and careworn" ("Naturally the Foundation Will Bear Your Expenses"), or the "loud noon of cities" and "children strewn on steps" ("Ambulances") to be found throughout Britain today, and they comment on the "split level shopping" and "bleak high-risers" ("Going, Going") marking the horizons of most English towns and cities. A few phrases in "At Grass" evoke the whole British obsession with "horseracing and betting." Larkin devotes an entire poem to the workingmen's store, contrasting rather elaborately the "cheap clothes"—suggestive of the "workday world of those / Who leave at dawn low terraced homes / Timed for factory, yard and site"—with the evidence nearby of a more exotic fantasy world: "Modes For Night: / . . . Lemon, sapphire, moss-green, rose / Bri-Nylon Baby-Dolls and Shorties" ("The Large Cool Store"). And in still another poem, he characterizes a hospital unmistakably urban: "All round it close-ribbed streets rise and fall. . . . / . . .short terraced streets / Where kids chalk games, and girls with hair-dos fetch/ Their separates from the cleaners" ("The Building"). Even billboard advertising merits a poem:

> In frames as large as rooms that face all ways
> And block the ends of streets with giant loaves,
> Screen graves with custard, cover slums with praises
> Of motor-oil and cuts of salmon. . . . ("Essential Beauty")

Perhaps even more than these outdoor settings, the domestic interiors of Larkin's poetry suggest current, if not ultramodern, life in Britain. The houses of his poems contain television, the Beatles' first LP, "the drier and the electric fire," "the hall to paint," and packets of old programs and letters. In "Mr. Bleaney" he captures the ennui of the seedy rented room by noting the "Flowered curtains, thin and frayed" which "Fall to within five inches of the sill, / Whose window shows a strip of building land, / Tussocky, littered." In "Home is so Sad" he again evokes tawdriness when the reader is urged to "Look at the pictures and the cutlery, / The music in the piano stool. / That vase." And piano-bench music itself becomes the subject of "Love Songs in Age," where Larkin distinguishes the covers of the sheet music: "One bleached from lying in a sunny place, / One marked in circles by a vase of water, / One mended. . . ." All such details suggest the kind of living quarters familiar to the average Englishman of town or city, and help make Larkin's poems basically urban and modern in character.

Even those poems not set in town or city display a countryside in close proximity to centers of population and likely to be frequented by people either moving from city to city or only briefly removed from their suburban homes. The speaker in "Church Going," though we find him in a small country church, frequently reminds us that his stay there is only temporary. Besides his bicycle and cycle-clips, and besides his sophisticated, agnostic perspective, he speaks of having come "through suburb scrub" and speculates on the churchgoing of other moderns like himself. In visiting the church, he seems to be visiting more than the temple of a perhaps outmoded faith; he seems a visitor also to a whole round of rural life about to disappear entirely. Likewise the speaker in "Myxomatosis" seems only a visitor to the countryside, poking the rabbit with his walking stick and speaking as a city man about a disease itself symbolic of modern science's incursion into rural life. In "Show Saturday," while the speaker may celebrate the survival of the traditional country show, he cannot help mentioning the trucks and vans, "the cars [jamming] the narrow lanes," or the fact that however attentive to the show its participants may be, the simplicity of the scene belies the complexity of the "local lives" to which they will soon return, a complexity owing partly to the age in which they live.

A scene of similar respite from the business of modern living appears in "To the Sea," where Larkin lovingly describes the ritual of sea-bathing, which has attracted generations of Englishmen. "[H]alf an annual pleasure, half a rite," such seagoing represents a necessary link between the contemporary Britisher and his ancient forebears. But the description here includes transistor radios, rusty cans, and candy-wrappers, which contribute to the speaker's sense of colorful pilgrimage. At day's end these pilgrims, like those in "Show Saturday," head for their homes in family cars. If for Larkin the happy human community can overshadow the "eternal note of sadness" caught by Matthew Arnold in contemplating the sea, he must describe its communal ritual with details unmistakably suggestive of a very modern Britain.

Interestingly the same kinds of details, including the bathers themselves, become the basis for anxiety and pessimism in "Going, Going," where Larkin envisions England becoming the "first slum of Europe" due to growing population, spreading towns and suburbs, and pollution. Citing many examples of contemporary Britain's destruction of her natural beauties, he climaxes his list by trailing off, "And when / You try to get near the sea / In summer. . . ." The crowds of bathers and their paraphernalia, those picturesque details of the other poem, become the ugly foreshadowing of an England to come. However, these two poems suggest not so much Larkin's love or hatred of sea-bathing crowds, or his shift or inconsistency of attitude toward them, as his tendency to give his poems unmistakably current settings.

Perhaps nowhere in his poetry is such a setting more evident than in those poems having to do with travel. That none of these deals with travel outside England—except the caustic "Naturally the Foundation Will Bear Your Expenses"—and that none is set outside England—but for another satiric exception, "Posterity"—reflects Larkin's loyalty to his country. His characters travel only within England, and usually by rail. In several poems the journey by train and references to rail travel operate almost emblematically, to represent life's journey and a glimpse of British life. Where for Chaucer the pilgrimage served such a purpose, and for many eighteenth- and nineteenth-century novelists—Fielding, Dickens, and George Eliot come immediately to mind—the coach ride through village and countryside gave a broad picture of English life, Larkin's pilgrim rides the train. In "Dockery and Son" he is riding home after visiting his old college. While the poem mainly concerns his meditations about the visit, Larkin has him awaken at the "fumes / And furnace-glares of Sheffield," eat "an awful pie" at the Sheffield station, and stand on the platform watching "the ranged / Joining and parting lines." Likewise, in "I Remember, I Remember," a train trip—this time through Coventry, the place of his birth—becomes an occasion for the Larkin character to reflect on his life as it has evolved.

The most explicit use of the train trip, though, where the speaker is made to consider what he sees as he travels, comes in "The Whitsun Weddings," one of Larkin's most striking and most effective

poems. Here the pilgrim, traveling on a Whitsun holiday toward
London from a northern English town (perhaps Hull), describes his
journey with much detail concerning the interior of the train, the
countryside, and especially the wedding parties his train picks up
through numerous stations along the way. The specifics include the
hot cushions and buttoned carriage-cloth of the railway car, the
"canals with floatings of industrial froth" marking the Lincolnshire
landscape, and the "perms, / The nylon gloves and jewellery-
substitutes, / The lemons, mauves, and olive-ochres" of the girls
from the weddings. All of these things, plus the account of approaching London ("Its postal districts packed like squares of
wheat"), help give the poem a basic contemporaneousness, though,
as noted before, Larkin's postwar setting tends more toward tawdriness than urbaneness.

Like the places in Larkin's poems, the people in them contribute
to this quality of concrete realism. Like many earlier novelists and
like John Betjeman, whom he so admires, Larkin has a keen eye for
the details of people, as well as things and places, and his poems
offer a remarkably wide range of minor figures behind their
speakers and narrators. Where in "The Whitsun Weddings" he
notes the newlyweds, in another poem he shows a young bride on
the day after her joyful wedding night, wondering if her happiness
can last ("Wedding Winds"), while in yet another ("Afternoons")
he describes young mothers with their children in the park, where
"the wind / Is ruining their courting-places / That are still courting-places." Then there is Arnold, the married friend of the speaker
in "Self's the Man," who is middle-aged, "with nippers to wheel
round the house" and a mother-in-law. "Breadfruit," one of
Larkin's uncollected poems, first published in 1961, reviews the
pattern of male sexual fantasizing from youth to old age, pausing to
note the middle-aged husbands in "A mortgaged semi- with a silver
birch." Larkin's loving sensitivity to the plight of such men is
amusingly underscored in his introduction to *All What Jazz*, the
collection of his jazz reviews, where he imagines his readers as
"sullen fleshy inarticulate men, stockbrokers, sellers of goods, living
in thirty-year-old detached houses among the golf courses of Outer
London, husbands of aging and bitter wives . . . fathers of cold-
eyed lascivious daughters on the pill . . . and cannabis-smoking
jeans-and-bearded Stuart-haired sons."[3] He hopes his writing about
jazz will remind such readers of the sweet sounds of their hopeful
youth.

But, because time and what it brings are preoccupations for
Larkin, his poems allude to people of all ages, and in various
situations and activities. Besides referring to children as "nippers"
to be wheeled about, or as playmates at "swing and shovel" with
their mothers in the parks, he sees them on city streets watching a
passing ambulance or playing games, at home with toys and pets,
and at the beach learning to swim. Youthful figures appear as discotheque patrons ("Reasons for Attendance"), as young men setting
out from their hometowns for uncertain adulthood ("How
Distant"), and as "a couple of kids" presumably enjoying sexual
freedom denied to earlier generations ("High Windows"). Nor are
the middle-aged figures of his poems confined to disillusioned
husbands. In "Faith Healing" we see a crowd of aging women,
"[M]oustached in flowered frocks," desperately revealing that
"idiot child within them" hungry for affection and understanding.
And, more self-reliant but no less poignant are the speaker's mother
in "Reference Back," happy to have her son home for a brief stay,
the widow looking over the old sentimental songs in her piano
("Love Songs in Age"), the deceased Mr. Bleaney, or the various
characters populating the parks in "Toads Revisited." Even the
very old receive sustained attention in at least one poem, "The Old
Fools," where the sight of them in a rest home or a hospital inspires
the speaker to ponder the puzzle of aging.

Larkin's poetry crosses boundaries besides that of age. Its population ranges from the lower classes, remembered most pointedly in
the young rape victim and her attacker in "Deceptions," to the
presumably wealthy Warlock-Williams, whose invitation the
speaker in "Vers de Société" answers. Though Larkin's failure to
refer very often to either the very poor or the very rich may reflect
the economic realities of the British welfare state, and thus operate
as another mark of his contemporaneousness, his minor characters
are sufficiently distinguished on other bases besides wealth to
suggest a fairly broad spectrum of attitudes and positions even
within the British middle class. Notably different levels of schooling
and cultural refinement mark his background characters, from the
well-read crowd at Warlock-Williams's party or the concertgoers in
"Broadcast," to the semiliterate Titch Thomas disfiguring the
railway poster in "Sunny Prestatyn," and from the learned Oxford
Dons in "Livings" to the "uncle shouting smut" in "The Whitsun
Weddings." Larkin notices people in a variety of occupations, as
well. He comments on railway porters "larking with the mails"

("The Whitsun Weddings"), factory workers ("The Large Cool Store"), salesmen ("Livings," "Friday Night in the Royal Station Hotel"), seamen ("Livings"), and miners ("The Explosion"). While the appeal of his poems depends on the universality of the human issues with which they deal, it surely rests too on their breadth of reference to human and physical details.

At least a few of his poems seem especially to hinge on such breadth of reference. Indeed, accompanying the development of thought and feeling in each of these poems is a careful delineation of an entire way of life. Such a poem is "Here," which, Larkin has remarked, "is about the part of England I live in, though not, I suppose, about it in the full guidebook sense."[4] "Here" differs from a guidebook in its attention to those commonplace and perhaps dull details which usually escape the tourist's eye but are so vital to the native's sense of what it means to live there. The poem opens with a survey of the countryside south of the town, presumably Hull:

> . . . fields
> Too thin and thistled to be called meadows,
> . . . .
> . . . solitude
> Of skies and scarecrows, haystacks, hares and pheasants,
> And the widening river's slow presence,
> The piled gold clouds, the shining gull-marked mud,
> Gathers to the surprise of a large town.

Reaching the town, Larkin surveys its horizon of "domes and statues, spires and cranes," and characterizes its "cut-priced crowd, urban yet simple," whose neighborhoods present "terminate and fishy-smelling / Pastorals of ships up streets, the slave museum, / Tattoo-shops, consulates, grim head-scarfed wives." The "mortgaged half-built edges" of the town gradually blend into the wheat fields and isolated villages of the countryside, "where removed lives / Loneliness clarifies."

An equally panoramic view is presented in "Show Saturday," which moves quickly from event to event, and audience to audience, catching the spirit of the show and its importance to the people. We see the various animal and livestock competitions, wrestling matches, and foods and crafts displays—all amid a profusion of objects, people, and sounds. Larkin notes the clash of public announcements ("shatteringly loud") with "the quack of the man with pound notes round his hat / And a lit-up board" and the squeal of logs in the chainsawing contest. The colorful crowd includes judges, hawkers of all kinds, contestants, and scattered spectators: "Folks [sitting] about on bales / Like great straw dice . . . / The men with hunters, dog-breeding wool-defined women, / Children all saddle-swank, mugfaced middleaged wives / Glaring at jellies, husbands on leave from the garden— Watchful as weasels, car-tuning curt-haired sons." Like bathing in the sea, the show carries for all of these folk an unexamined ritual significance: "something they share / That breaks ancestrally each year into / Regenerate union."

In "MCMXIV" Larkin looks back at the last days of Edwardian innocence, before England's plunge into modern times. He begins by comparing the nonchalance of the first waves of enlistees, as shown in photographs—"Grinning as if it were all / An August Bank Holiday lark"—to the merriment of the cricket crowds at Kennington Oval. He then surveys some emblems of a way of life which, unknown to its participants, would suddenly disappear forever: the bleached blinds of closed shops; coins that have since passed out of circulation because of inflation or monetary shifts; the servant class; tidy gardens; "dark-clothed children at play / Called after kings and queens"; and "tin advertisements / For cocoa and twist." All of these represent for Larkin an irretrievable world-view and life-style. Indeed, so struck is he by the consequences of their passing that he purposely chose roman numerals, as on a tombstone, over the arabic, which he found almost too awful to contemplate and beyond the modest dimensions of his poem.[5] However modest, though, this quiet poem captures the essential feel of England in her last years of innocence and world supremacy in the twentieth century. Because such innocence permeated English life, Larkin has drawn upon the great and the obscure, in people and objects, to mourn its absence from his contemporary England.

II *Character and Situation*

To say that Larkin draws upon the concrete details of British life is not to say that these details are obscure to the non-British reader, or that a full understanding of them is required for Larkin's poems to make sense. The details he includes are hardly ever too restrictive to be grasped by any thoughtful reader of English. Scrupulously selected in part to avoid such restrictiveness, they suggest the British version of the stuff of life for most people today. If they lend a distinctive note of concreteness, realism, or locale to the poems, they do not contribute to the poems' complexity or obscurity; whatever complexity or obscurity Larkin can be credited or charged with depends upon the manner and direction of thought and feeling in the poems, not upon their incidental details of setting. In this respect he differs markedly from John Betjeman, who seems to thrive on loading his poems with the minutiae of social class, architecture, and historical era, and whose provincialism for his detractors and charm for his admirers depend upon such loading. In creating settings demonstrably but not obscurely British, Larkin more resembles Hardy, in whose poems universally human personality and problems subsume the Wessex locale and character.

The overwhelming majority of Larkin's poems are lyrics, showing a single, isolated speaker. And, but for a dozen-or-so exceptions, these lyric poems are organized around the developing thoughts and feelings of their speakers, rather than logical arguments or special occasions. Larkin's speakers themselves and the personal situations which inspire their musings suggest a less provincial appeal than Betjeman's poetry, but an appeal more contemporary than that of Hardy.

Perhaps most indicative of this difference between Larkin and both Betjeman and Hardy are those poems dealing with religion. While the problem of living in what one of Larkin's admirers has termed the "post post-Christian world"[6] is almost always implicit in his poetry, in a few of the poems we see characters especially plagued by that problem. Such a poem is the celebrated "Church Going," which helped make Larkin's reputation in England and America during the 1950s, and in which the speaker confronts the disparity between his professed unbelief in the sanctities of traditional Christianity and his own "gravitating" to that anachronistic center of such piety, the country church. Wavering between the playful cynicism which marked his late-adolescent rebellion against religion and a more recent despair and loneliness, he muses on the parodox of his own personality—freed from the shackles of superstition and conformity, yet enslaved by the limited perspective such freedom affords—and that of his contemporaries—bored and uninformed, without the hypocrisy and cant of professed religion, yet also without the solace, however illusory, which it long ago conferred upon believers.

If doubt has led to disbelief, the speaker finds such doubt and disbelief dubious gains in the face of the plaguing personal and metaphysical questions with which religion has at least tried to deal. The nineteenth-century skeptic, finding the traditional answers to such questions unsatisfactory, might hope that other more satisfying answers could be found. Thus a sort of cosmic hopefulness colored the writings of George Eliot, and cannot be said to have disappeared entirely from Arnold or even Hardy. But Larkin's speaker—puzzled, honest, and sincere—obviously lives in a more recent time, after most other answers have been found wanting and have been discarded, and when the questions themselves have come to be regarded as virtually unanswerable. Because their seeming unanswerability makes them all the more taunting, he can see only his and mankind's hunger for such answers.

Other poems show speakers caught in the same predicament. "High Windows," written almost twenty years later, shows not the still youthful, cycling churchgoer, but a speaker definitely middle-aged, comparing his envy of the apparent sexual freedom of today's youth—"everyone young going down the long slide / To happiness, endlessly"—with what he supposes was an earlier generation's envy of his own freedom from conventional religion: "*He and his lot will all go down the long slide / Like free bloody birds.*" The poem turns on his admitting that freedom from religious "bonds and gestures" has not freed him from the metaphysical questing, just as, by analogy, sexual freedom probably has not solved the mysteries of sexuality and human relations. Again the Larkin speaker comes off as thoughtful and honest, and as skeptical of the fruits of skepticism.

Even in "Water," a poem of Larkin's *Whitsun Weddings* period, we find the speaker speculating, significantly, on what sort of religion he would construct, "If I were called in." Obviously he is not being called in, and probably will not be. Nevertheless, his compulsion to imagine such a call and the religion he constructs as an answer suggest that, while not religious in any traditional sense, he feels as dissatisfied with his disbelief as with conventional dogma. As with "Church Going" and High Windows," we see a man sensitive to the possibility of religion, yet conditioned by at least a couple of generations of widespread scorn blending into indifference toward Christianity.

Larkin's characters are not very often explicitly concerned with their will to believe in an age in which belief has died. More frequently they are bothered by the corollary, and perhaps more unversally compelling, problem of the intimations of age and mortality they feel, and bothered in a characteristically midcentury fashion. A painful awareness of oncoming age figures in a number of poems, where, as in "High Windows," the Larkin speaker may meditate on the gulf between him and the young. But, where in that poem the gulf disappears in a wave of empathy, in "How Distant" the character develops the sense of his distance from "being young" by noting examples of youthful setting forth; he does so as one who understands the youthful temptation of escape to the unknown but who cannot return himself to such a state. Similarly, in "Sad Steps," the speaker notices the clarity of the moon—"(Stone-colored light sharpening the roofs below) / High and preposterous and separate"—but instead of interpreting this in traditional romantic fashion, he sees it as a reminder of youth, which, while still strong for some, can never return to him. Equally interesting, especially in comparison with "High Windows," is "Mr. Bleaney," a much earlier poem, where a much younger speaker, taking a room in a seedy rooming house, begins by scornfully asserting his superiority over Bleaney, the older, presumably unsuccessful, and recently deceased former occupant of the room, but ends with the horrible recognition of his own vulnerability to time and failure.

In later poems, Larkin's undoubtedly middle-aged speaker more explicitly connects his sense of aging with his fear of dying. In "Vers de Société" he debates going to a party likely to be a bore, but after meditating on the folly and pretentiousness of social games he decides to go, and justifies this decision with a revealing argument:

> Only the young can be alone freely.
> The time is shorter now for company,
> And sitting by a lamp more often brings
> Not peace, but other things.

Relatedly the speaker in "Money," again a middle-aged bachelor, sadly observes the similarity between his having saved money and having measured out his life Prufrock style. "You can't put off being young until you retire," he sadly concludes.

Yet, this concern with dying and death is no recent development for Larkin, since even in *The Less Deceived* we find at least two poems, "Absences" and "Going," devoted to death. In the one the speaker imagines what the natural scenes he observes will be without him to observe them, while in the other, written probably in the 1940s, he disbelievingly questions his experience as he becomes one of the dying, in a manner reminiscent of Emily Dickinson.

The Larkin character can be bothered by many things besides thoughts of old age and death. In several poems he debates with himself over the virtue or curse of work. The best-known of these poems are "Toads" and its sequel, "Toads Revisited." "Toads" finds him considering first the reasons why he ought not to let work "squat" on his life, and then avoiding the logical outcome of this line of thought by falling back on a moralistic denunciation of those managing to survive without working.

In "Toads Revisited" he again confronts the question of his work, but strays even less than before from his resolve to keep working. This time he compares his lot only with the various unemployed "characters" he sees in the park—which certainly begs the question—and returns quickly to his assumption that somehow working is better for him:

> No, give me my in-tray,
> My loaf-haired secretary,
> My shall-I-keep-the-call-in-Sir:
> What else can I answer,
>
> When the lights come on at four
> At the end of another year?

This tussle between the lures of dull security and risky excape appears more broadly in "Poetry of Departures," where, having confessed his attraction to "chucking" everything—possessions, job, morality—the speaker ends by attacking such escape as deliberate and artificial, a charge equally applicable to his decision to stay stuck.

If such expressions of discontent seem less than wholly sincere, or at least insufficient to effect an escape, elsewhere Larkin reveals situations of discontent from which there appears no escape. There the character recalls that his now uncomfortable lot once appeared attractive and that he more or less freely chose it. Such disillusionment is expressed in "A Study of Reading Habits," where the speaker, whom Larkin has characterized as an "ordinary man,"[7] recounts having, as a child, identified with the hero of his redings, as an adolescent having seen himself in the role of the villains he read about, but now, as an adult—because only "the dude/ Who lets the girl down before/The hero arrives" or "the chap/

Who's yellow and keeps the store" reminds him very much of himself—generally avoiding reading) Such disillusionment with oneself is treated more seriously in "Sympathy in White Major," where the speaker looks back regretfully on a lifetime of trying to help others. Describing his purity of motives as "whiteness," he ruefully admits that his success was at best qualified and that, anyway, "White is not my favorite color."

The chief area of disappointment and self-doubt for the Larkin character is his relationships with others. Typically Larkin's speaker sees himself as a failure in love, friendship, or his relations to society; he spends much time analyzing the nature of this failure and the extent of his responsibility. The Larkin lover is a would-be lover. In the ironically titled "Wild Oats" we see him recalling an early and protracted love affair with a girl whom he chose to pursue instead of her more attractive friend, thinking, with characteristic self-disdain, that he would have a better chance with the less attractive girl. He retains the memories of seven years of letters and meetings, degenerating toward a rather bitter separation, and a couple of pictures of her friend, "a bosomy English rose." Having compromised to gain what he saw as the surer mate, he finds himself, even many years after their separation, wondering at his seeming inability to love or to attract love. In another poem, "Maiden Name," the Larkin romancer meditates on the implications of a former girl friend's abandoning her maiden name when she married. From his almost vicious musings on her former name emerges the sense that he himself feels abandoned, and that his claims of "faithfulness" to the memory of her as she was represent only the outpourings of lonely desperation. And, in "Latest Face," he shyly speculates on the possibilities of love with a girl he has just seen for the first time. Characteristically anticipating difficulties in their relating to each other, he prefers not to pursue the possibility.

Even when established in a relationship, the Larkin lover is uncomfortable. Such is the case in "Lines on a Young Lady's Photograph Album," where the speaker examines photos from his girl friend's family album. As he comments on the pictures, the peculiar nature of photography, and the difficulty of preserving a moment of reality, we get the sense of a lover on his way out, desperate to retain some remembrance of the girl. Rather than living in the present with her, he is forced to consider her past, a rather imperfect means of having her, and to imagine his future without her. Even in the poem added to the new edition of *The*

North Ship ("Waiting for breakfast, while she brushed her hair"),
where the speaker is secure in his relationship with a lover, we find
him torn between the demands of that relationship and something
which lies outside it, in this case his desire to write. His muse, he
fears, envies his girl friend. Having been unable to write, he considers abandoning the relationship in favor of his art. Again love
proves a detriment to happiness.

That the Larkin speaker never marries is perhaps a symptom or a
result of this unhappiness. His unmarried state scarcely gives him
satisfaction. Rather, we see him, in several poems, wondering and
ultimately doubting that his decision to remain single—if it was *his*
decision—was wise. The speaker in "Self's the Man" compares his
life with his married friend Arnold's. After moving through a moral
examination of their lives and concluding, at least to his satisfaction,
that Arnold is no less selfish than he, he turns to the question of self-
satisfaction, deciding that "I'm a better hand / At knowing what I
can stand / Without them sending a van," but adding, "Or I suppose I can." This final hint of doubt brings him back to his initial
need for vindication; he still feels obliged to justify not having a
wife and family, and this feeling itself signals serious dissatisfaction.

In much the same way the speaker in "Dockery and Son," upon
learning that a college classmate has a son in college, feels obligated
to justify, even to rationalize, his failure to marry and have a son of
his own. Though Larkin has insisted that this is not a poem of
regret,[8] the speaker's speculating on Dockery's motives in having a
son ("how / Convinced he was he should be added to!")—as if
Dockery necessarily procreated in so deliberate a fashion—his disparaging of the motive—"Why did he think adding meant increase? / To me it was dilution"—and his characterizing the
son—of whom he knows nothing except his age—as presumably un-
grateful and returning "all a son's harsh patronage," remind us of
the other speaker's disparagement of Arnold's life, a disparagement
suggestive more of personal disappointment and sour grapes than
objectivity.

The same syndrome of at least partial regret for what has failed to
develop in personal relations comes in "Maiden Name" and in the
seventh selection of *XX Poems* ("Since the majority of me"), for the
speaker in each talks of a broken relationship, perhaps a love affair,
so as to suggest a sense of loss despite the fact that the break was a
mutual decision. If the speakers in these poems avoid the rationalizing of the other two, they nevertheless display the same doubt, self-
criticism, and loneliness.

In fact, loneliness, or at least the sense of being left out, colors almost all of Larkin's speakers and their personal situations. The Larkin speaker is almost always aloof and at most an unparticipating spectator at the rooted lives and pleasures of others. Two poems illustrate this tendency with special poignancy. In one, "Reasons for Attendance," the speaker finds himself outside a discotheque, watching the youthful dancers inside. Presumably older, he ponders why he should be outside, but then questions the assumption that being coupled with someone leads to happiness. Concluding that he prefers his independence, while they obviously prefer their mutual dependence, he decides that each position is satisfactory for him who holds it, "If no one has misjudged himself. Or lied." As in "Self's the Man," the speaker's qualification of what seems a standoff between opposing arguments tips the balance in favor of that which he lacks.

In "Places, Loved Ones," much the same arguments are rehearsed, this time in terms of the whole issue of home and family. But, the speaker moves beyond the defense of independence to admit that, having missed such things, he feels obligated to believe as if what he settled for suited him. Having reached middle age without the ties of family or home, he sees himself victimized by the rationalizations arising from his situation, and therefore lacking in will to attempt any correction of that situation.

So aloof is the Larkin character that he can rarely share even the most commonplace pleasures of others. "Spring" finds him noting carefully the quality which that season confers on nature and people, but concluding wearily that those, like himself, who can see nature best and need her consolation most stand beyond her power to gladden or console. In view of this inability to escape personal dissatisfaction, the speaker's admission in "Coming" that on longer evenings heralding spring's coming even he, for whom childhood usually represents only "forgotten boredom," testifies more to the superhuman powers of nature than to the probability of his uniting very deeply or permanently with his fellow men in their enjoyment of nature. It is at most a fragile happiness he can feel at such times.

The poem "Age" puts this aloofness in larger perspective. There the speaker meditates on a curious dilemma. On the one hand, he has remained distant from his era, and thus capable of objectively assessing it and his possible imprint on it, but, on the other hand, such distance has prevented his being able to see either the age or his imprint very clearly. While he poses an irresolvable issue, it is significant that again we see a man at a point of his life where a sense of personal achievement is valued, but his situation—in this case his chosen distance—precludes his having that satisfaction. Regardless of the merits of such distance—the individuality, nonconformity, or integrity it may confer—— like the various kinds of freedom chosen or exhibited by other Larkin characters (freedom from the bonds of religion, from marriage, from all ties), it has proven insufficient to his needs. But, as the poems on work suggest, we are not to suppose that proximity or greater conformity would necessarily have proven more satisfactory.

III   *Questions and Issues*

Much of Philip Larkin's artistry rests in his ability to concretize—through setting, personality, and diction—many of the questions which have perplexed man almost since his beginning but which in modern times have become the province principally of academicians. In this he especially resembles Thomas Hardy. Because Larkin's poetry reflects his determination to remove poetry from the sterile academy and to speak to a wider range of readers than many of his modernist predecessors, it reflects, too, his faith in the common reader to recognize and respond to traditional philosophical concerns when stripped of undue abstractness and pretentious labels. To examine, even briefly, the ideological content of Larkin's poems is thus to undo what he has done so skillfully. But, because analysis necessarily robs such philosophical issues of the immediacy and appeal given them by a poetic context, it nicely suggests the advantage of such a context, as well as the poet's skill in drawing it.

As the earlier discussion of Larkin's characters and their situations should have suggested, a major consideration of his poetry is Time. In this he recalls many of the giants of modern literature—among them Proust, Faulkner, Yeats, and Woolf. Yet none of these has appealed to so broad an audience as Larkin. Many of the poems discussed earlier show specific characters dealing with the passing of their lives and the accompanying feelings of inadequacy and dissatisfaction. In a few other poems, where the speaker is less individualized and more reliable at least than Larkin's rationalizers, the question of Time itself is treated explicitly. In one of these the wholly reliable speaker, who can perhaps be thought of as Larkin himself, remarks that Time is man's element. "Days are where we live," he comments, as he goes on to note how answering the question of where else man might live requires death; life necessarily means Time.

But, does Time exist in any real sense? In a manner reminiscent of Aristotle and Augustine, Larkin confronts the Riddle of Time, that element in which we seem to move in the present. In "Triple Time," he speaks of the present as "a time unrecommended by event," yet he notes how, ironically, this is both the future once dreamed of and the past soon to be recalled with nostalgia or regret. While serving as a depository for our dreams and our rationalizations, the present moment is but an "empty street," since memory and imagination cannot operate on it. Its emptiness and the frustration attendant upon our repeatedly discovering that emptiness form the subject of "Next, Please," where Larkin compares our habitual anticipation to sitting on a bluff waiting for the ship to come in loaded with compensations for past failures and disappointments. Just as this ship proves to be an illusion, so does the presumed time of its arrival, which immediately turns from anticipated future to regretted past. With understanding Larkin catches here the emotion attending man's inability to be simplistically rooted in the present. Those faculties separating us from the lower animals—our general rationality, but especially our memory and imagination—undo us, as they merely make us more frustrated than we would be without them. Yet, as Larkin suggests, man continues to hope for a measurable and durable present, occupying an illusory vantage-point much like the "specious present" of modern philosophers. If life means Time, Time means the almost constant alteration of illusion and disillusionment.

Man's tendency to be deluded and then to be disappointed operates as an assumption in most of Larkin's poems. In none is so extreme a case offered as in "Deceptions," originally titled "The Less Deceived" until Larkin appropriated that title for the collection in which it appeared. In this poem he meditates on a young girl's account of being conscripted for prostitution and raped, taken from Matthew Mayhew's *London Labour and the London Poor*. Sympathetic with the physical and psychic abuse undergone by the girl, especially in the moralistic context of Victorian London, he chooses, nevertheless, to compare her suffering with her attacker's self-deception. If she was victimized by his sexual brutality, he was the victim of the illusion of total and permanent satisfaction which the attack seemed to promise. In a characteristic distortion of the Keats ode, Larkin takes the man, by no means a lover, off of the urn

and has him complete his ravishment of the maiden, only to discover that the joy he sought was illusory. Though the girl cannot be
consoled for her various pains, she harbored no delusions as to what
was happening. Because Larkin thus uses the rapist's lust as an
emblem of all human desires, his sense of shared self-deception
allows him to go beyond pity for the girl or indignation against the
rapist. For Larkin the cycle of sexual desire, momentary fulfillment,
and renewed frustration illustrates handily man's general predicament.

In another poem, "Dry Point," he describes more graphically the
tempting illusion and disillusionment plaguing man in his sexuality.
Significantly dubbing sex a "time-honored irritant," he goes on to
describe the endless process of pressure which forces toward climax
and the resulting emptiness. Since sex is but the most pervasive
desire bothering desire-ridden man, logic suggests that the ideal
would be not so much a permanent fulfillment of desire—since that
dream is what constantly teases us into dissatisfaction—as a state
from which desire is barred. Yet, as Larkin suggests, such a state
would be, from a human standpoint, not only desireless but un-
desirable, a state of death. In all of his poems dealing with time and
desire, he implicitly posits the paradox: though seeking relief from
time and desire, man can think and dream only in these terms. To
Larkin being undeceived about the illusory nature of desire and
time makes a person only less unhappy. Because such awareness
differs markedly from the happiness we would have, even the most
undeceived among us are periodically subject to the distractions of
desire.

Given the bleakness of reality as Larkin views it, man's proneness
to illusion is at least a mixed blessing, since it affords him temporary
escape. One critic has described human nature as seen by Larkin as
the attitude that "a bird in the bush is worth two in the hand."[9]
Certainly the tendency to assume, or at least to hope, that somehow
future time will alter the unsatisfying present suggests a persistent
disregard for the implications of past experience. The Larkin
character not only ignores the present, partly because he cannot see
it for what it is, but generally when thinking of the future he blocks
out the past, and vice versa. If resolved to hope, he ignores
probabilities suggested by the past; when resolved to regret, he ignores the potential openness of his future.

Of course, this extremely limited time perspective suggests
another tenet of the human situation as seen by Larkin: the difficul-

ty, indeed the inherent disadvantage, of viewing things objectively. So limited is man's sense of perspective that he is unable to know what he should know and what he should not know. This inability is shown pointedly in "Whatever Happened?", where the speaker notes how immediately after some mishap memory begins editing and placing the experience in a perspective which, if anything, distorts its personal meaning. Comparing the resulting memory after a day or so to a photograph and a still later impression to a map, he describes the seemingly unavoidable process of abstracting, which leaves a very untrustworthy shadow of the actual experience. The price paid for such a clear outline is, of course, distance, while proximity, which survives in nightmarish images, only adds to the confusion. Larkin's point here is that man must settle for the insufficient objective or the confusing subjective; he cannot have the advantages of both. And behind all of this is Time, always turning the almost graspable present into the elusive past.

Larkin's concern with a human world caught up in time, desire, and disappointment connects him with the whole line of western philosophy dealing with the distinction between the ideal and the real. His peculiar emphasis upon this distinction has prompted one critic succinctly to label Larkin's viewpoint as "Platonism turned over or inside out,"[10] since the true Platonist reality, which is ulterior, becomes fantasy for the characters of Larkin's poems. However, the same critic, while noting Larkin's disbelief in any sort of Platonic Ideal, notes that such an ideal exists for Larkin in that he sees it as essential to the human state; we seem unable to live without positing impossible, unworkable ideals.[11] Because Larkin, despite knowing better, presumably shares this proneness to idealize in the face of unpleasant or unrewarding reality, his attitude toward the idealizing tendency of his characters, or of mankind in general, can only be that of profound sympathy. Because Larkin's realism involves a hard look at life, because reality for him does not give cause for joy, he cannot deride the very natural bent toward escape-through-idealizing.

In fact, he can respond with wonder at the ingenuity with which men color reality. In "The Large Cool Store," for instance, after remarking the contrast between the workday fashions and the "Modes for Night" in the working-class store, he concludes that the common man's erecting a fantasy world shows "How separate and unearthly love is, / Or women are, or what they do, | Or in our young unreal wishes / Seem to be." Just as the display of cheap nightgowns expresses man's desire for all which is "synthetic, new / And natureless in ecstasies," so does advertising appeal, in Larkin's view, not so much to base instinct, as to that understandable desire to transcend the everyday world's limits.

In "Sunny Prestatyn," when he confronts a travel poster for a second-rate resort featuring the customary beckoning girl in swimsuit and various additions to her face and form by graffiti artists, he finds himself torn between the romantic lure of beach, girl, and sunshine, and the realization of its unreality and ultimate ridiculousness. Skeptical about the poster itself and therefore sympathetic to the realistic scorn prompting the obscene additions, he seems equally skeptical about the advantages of destroying all such fantasies. While the graphic description of the additions shows his identification with the graffitist, he seems to see in such indignation not just anger against the manipulative advertiser, but bitter regret that the dream exploited in the poster cannot be fulfilled. The graffitist thus expresses annoyance with himself for entertaining such wishes and with reality for failing to fulfill them. If the poster appeals to our fantasies, it can do so only because we live in a world mostly cold, plain, lonely, and offering only temporary pleasure. Larkin, like the graffitist Titch Thomas, knows too much to be fooled by the poster in the railway station; but he also knows too much to believe that no succumbing to the poster's lure and not getting on the train for Prestatyn will make him much happier. A not unregretful conviction colors his conclusion that the poster girl was "too good for this world." The "Fight Cancer" poster replacing her hardly offers more comfort.

Advertising figures prominently in another Larkin poem, "Essential Beauty," which traces the disparity between the illusory world of billboards, "these sharply-pictured groves / Of how life should be," and the imperfection of real existence, "where nothing's made / As new or washed quite clean," and concludes with the sober facts of sickness, old age, and death, which advertising rarely recognizes.

One critic has found man more pathetic in Larkin's world of modern goods and advertising than in Hardy's, owing to the greater transiency of the places and things familiar to contemporary man. She claims that the "affront" of life is doubly compounded by the ideal which modern life presents: "first because of the vacuousness of its offering which proclaims 'pure form' and screens graves not with heaven but with custard, but also because of its extreme materialism which submits the ideal to the trial of reality where, too easily, it is found false."[12] Larkin's man is more readily disappointed because forced to worship shallower idols. The old sense of stability to places and things has given way to the "sleasy quality of objects built not to last."[13]

Certainly in speaking of cheap nightgowns, edibles in throwaway containers, and other mass-produced goods, Larkin has surrounded his characters with a less stable environment than the rural buildings or impersonal Nature surrounding Hardy's sufferers. In one sense, we may see man amid such temporal objects as a much more pathetic creature than Hardy's victim of a chance-filled cosmos. But, it is possible to exaggerate the difference in viewpoint between the two poets. Whether Larkin sees man as actually worse off than in Hardy's day is questionable. If the goods surrounding his characters are, in fact, "sleasy," he generally ignores this quality, emphasizing only their failure to satisfy man's ultimate longings. Likewise the advertising of such goods—though it may be looked on as pernicious—is not viewed so by Larkin. Instead, he sees it as symptomatic of modern man's need for fantasy-fulfillment, a continuation of the same need earlier generations expressed through myth and religion.

Larkin's own recorded comments on "Essential Beauty" are instructive, for, while admitting to having scorned billboards as "vulgar and meretricious" when young, he says that maturity has caused him to like them, to find them "rather pathetic, rather moving . . . as if they were infinitely debased forms of the platonic essense."[14] This refusal to adopt a superior attitude to them or to condemn them or the goods they advertise probably relates to his refusal to condemn as foolish the people who are inspired by them. Though one may view premodern man as having had greater consolation in his sorrow, Larkin might see this view itself as an idealization of a past that never was. And, even if Hardy's man could sustain his illusions longer, Larkin's can be conditioned to accept more gracefully the disappointments which, both poets agree, life inevitably brings.

Two other issues closely related to the ideal / real distinction figure prominently in Larkin's writings. One of these, the problem of impermanence, has already been touched on. Our helplessness amidst the flux in our lives Larkin illustrates in "Talking in Bed," where he notes how such talk, seemingly emblematic of honesty between two people, disintegrates into either strained silence or deceptive chatter with the passing of time: "Nothing shows why / At this unique distance from isolation / It becomes still more difficult to find / Words at once true and kind, / Or not true and not unkind." The opportunity for ideal intimacy gradually fades; in its place comes either cruelty or dishonesty.

This failure to maintain so promising a situation is treated more abstractly in "Home is so Sad," where the speaker projects his own sadness onto his home, which has not changed. What has changed is the people, including himself, who lived there. The idea of home here is what people try to create in establishing their homes—"A joyous shot at how things ought to be"—yet the speaker, looking at the furnishings of his home, must sadly judge the shot "Long fallen wide." Again Larkin depicts the human drive toward realizing an ideal relationship failing through the transitory nature of reality. Situations fail to satisfy not only because they are inherently imperfect, but because no matter how nearly perfect, they never last. World War I catches the people in "MCMXIV" unaware as their peaceful way of life surrenders to time and events beyond them. For all of his calculations at choosing a girl not beyond his range, the speaker in "Wild Oats" recalls how, by some mysterious process, their relationship deteriorated. And, even the respite from care which the character in "Arrivals, Departures" looks forward to each evening is undermined by his fear that it may not last the night.

Because change is a disturbing staple in the Larkin world, the old question of freedom and responsibility often comes up in his poems. We have mentioned the various rationalizers who try to avoid responsibility for their failures. More reliably the speaker in "As Bad as a Mile" explores the possibility of deterministic patterns by considering the implications of missing the wastebasket with an apple core. Rejecting the notion of bad luck as too simplistic and question-begging, he develops the possibility of inherent failure enveloping the total situation, perhaps as far back even as the unraised hand and the unbitten apple. With biblical overtones, he deals with man's inborn proneness to error, to suggest a secular version of Original Sin.

In a more recent poem, "This Be The Verse," the Larkin speaker exhibits a similar awareness when he begins—"They fuck you up, your mum and dad. / They may not mean to but they do."—and goes on to speak of the accretion of hereditary traits and tendencies, a genetic and psychological falling away from some original state of grace. While in neither poem is Larkin offering a definitive answer to the puzzle of human shortcomings, in each he reminds the reader that we do fail, probably more often than we succeed. The plausibility of the explanations he toys with in these poems rests in their recognition not only of man's failings but of his limited self-control. Though we like to think of ourselves as masters of our selves and our fates, experience, Larkin is saying, suggests that either we exercise that mastery most foolishly or, more likely, our control is extremely limited. Neither possibility supports a very heroic view of man.

IV   *Assumptions and Values*

Probably the single most dominant impression emerging from Larkin's poems is that life is neither long nor sweet. This has caused one critic to remark that "English poetry has never been so persistently out in the cold. . . . Frost is a perennial boy, Hardy a fighter, by comparison."[15] Despite the plain-speaking of his poems, which places him technically in the Wordsworth tradition, the assumptions behind his portrayal of life differ markedly from those of Wordsworth and the other romantics.

Larkin's insistence in most of his poems on the bleakness of life is itself a tacit recommendation to his readers to look with honesty at the reality around them. Some have questioned why, given his view of existence, he even bothers to write. One critic has seen at the center of his poetry "The tension between the urge to write and the sense of its pointlessness."[16] Another sees Larkin recognizing the problem for the writer who rejects imagination for drab truth, that "there is not much pleasure to be got from the truth as anyone sees it," but goes on to note how Larkin apparently enjoys fully revealing such dullness and rejecting any sort of false redemption through imagination.[17] One might go even further and say that for Philip Larkin writing seems almost a test of his own honesty, to remind himself that, for the most part, he can look at things squarely, without flinching and without telling lies. While rarely didactic in form, his poems remind us of the moral and intellectual imperative of such vision.

This wryly stoic honesty appears in many contexts. In "Next, Please," having rejected that long-awaited ship loaded with compensations for our lives' disappointments, he does not hesitate to continue the metaphor in a grim conclusion: "Only one ship is seeking us, a black- / sailed unfamiliar, towing at her back / A huge and birdless silence." This refusal to allow even a neutral base for any romantic reversal can be seen, too, in "Take One Home for the Kiddies," where he dispels the romantic myth of children and childhood. Rather than a time of strong sensibility, childhood here appears a time of obliviousness to feelings. One moment the children in the poem beg their mother to buy them a pup "to keep"; the next they glibly turn the pup's death into an occasion for "playing funerals." If real mourners engage in undue sentimentality, they at least suffer a real sense of loss. While for Larkin funerals may be a more realistic form of play than lavishing affection on a dog, that the children, in fact, relish the funeral situation itself—"Living toys are something novel, / But it soon wears off somehow"—suggests an insensitivity contrary to the precocity of feeling often attributed to them.

This same skepticism about the innocence and virtue of children can be found in Larkin's 1959 review of a book on the lore and language of childhood, which amusingly begins: "It was that verse about becoming again as a little child that caused the first sharp waning of my Christian sympathies. If the kingdom of Heaven could be entered only by those fulfilling such a condition I know I should be unhappy there."[18] For the remainder of his essay he characterizes children as generally dull-witted and warns against exaggerating their merits or the shortcomings of adults. "Children are bound to be inferior to adults or there is no incentive to grow up," he observes.[19]

Larkin is equally intent on deromanticizing Nature and man's place in it. For one thing, he doesn't talk about Nature very often. His difference from Hardy in this regard reflects a difference in background and era: where in Hardy we see a poet regretting that Nature is not as Wordsworth promised, with Larkin we find a man so removed from the nineteenth-century debate over Nature that he has never thought to take seriously the notion of Nature as imminent or benign. That Nature, especially in the spring, can be outwardly beautiful he would not deny. But that man can derive any consolation from the patterns and cycles of the natural world he regards as a foolish notion.

This insistence on a realistic viewpoint is especially evident in "The Trees," where he takes a hard look at springtime and its meaning for man. If Hardy can no longer believe in the benign message he once attributed to natural beauty, Larkin never could. He exhibits a fearful fascination with such a possibility, but remains wholly unable to accept it; he approaches the budding trees from a decidedly agnostic background. Thus he cautiously qualifies his descriptions: the trees coming into leaf he compares to "something *almost* being said" (my italics) and concludes only that "they *seem* to say / Begin afresh." This unwavering disbelief is further revealed by his examination, in the middle stanza, of how the trees create the illusion of rebirth:

> Is it that they are born again
> And we grow old? No, they die too.
> Their yearly trick of looking new
> Is written down in rings of grain.

According to Larkin, if Nature can be said to be up to anything, it is trickery or sleight-of-hand, but he hesitates even to conclude this about the trees. Rather, he suggests that such readings are themselves probably the tricks of unreliable imagination.

All we can know is that Nature operates in cyclical patterns, while man exists in a linear-time dimension. This difference alone prevents man from being in harmony with Nature. Significantly, most of the poems concentrating to any appreciable extent on the natural scene are set in spring, when the disparity between Nature's powers of rejuvenation and seeming immortality, and man's aging and mortality, initiates a painful ritual for the speaker. There may be validity in one critic's notion that Larkin's insistence only on "blind cycles" in Nature comments more negatively than Hardy's blind Will on the dignity of man in the cosmos,[20] as if the despair of Hardy's "Hap" were taken one step further.

As much as he recommends an honest look at the world and people around us, Larkin admires honest self-appraisal. This is clear from the series of ironic rationalizers already discussed, each of whom backs off from what emerge as rather obvious implications of his thinking. Honesty about oneself, though difficult to achieve and perhaps impossible to maintain constantly, forms the basis of commendable behavior for Larkin. The young man in "Church Going" gains the reader's trust not only through his low-keyed and sympathetic appraisal of the traditional religion he can no longer accept, but through his gentle deprecation of himself, "bored and uninformed." Similarly the speaker in "If, My Darling" wins our amused sympathy by his, if anything, excessive modesty. Shamefacedly admitting to having tricked his girl friend by respectable outward behavior and appearance, he insists that were she to jump into his head she would find a mental house infested with betrayal and meaningless terminology. His decision not to reveal himself entirely reflects some concern for how such disillusioning might hurt his darling; because of self-awareness, as well as the sophisticated wit with which it is demonstrated, this does not seem a rationalization of baser motives. Though he ignores his own better motives and probably overplays the shallow regions of his psyche, the poem implies the greater wisdom of underrating than overrating one's virtues. For this same reason Larkin satirizes his would-be biographer in "Posterity" as a fool for expecting his subject to be much more than "One of those old-type natural fouled-up guys."

Given Larkin's stress on the recognition and acceptance of ordinariness in a world too prone to distort ordinary reality into the extraordinary, clear vision would seem to be the most important means to survival in such a world. In "Born Yesterday" he wishes for the new daughter of a friend not the romantic dream of beauty, innocence, and love—which strikes him as an extremely long shot—but "an average of talents" and a vigilant, flexible habit of mind, as requisites to a modicum of happiness. The formula for success contained in the poem is characteristically negative, couched more in terms of what the child must avoid and must not have, than of positive attributes. The tone of his wishes for her suggests one who has thoughtfully considered various attitudes toward life and his chances in it, and has decided on a course at once realistic and practical. Having realized his own limitations and the unlikelihood of life honoring the egocentricity of any individual, he wishes for the infant mainly that same good sense from her very beginning, to assure the most nearly smooth path in an existence bound to produce some rough spots.

Though such a habit of mind figures as preeminent among virtues in Larkin's world, he would not advocate coldheartedness. On the contrary, the many poems in which he reveals his own weakness for such dreams as success, freedom, rebirth, and sexual ecstasy suggest a basic sympathy for the weak and erring. Larkin comes off as a man who knows from painful experience how difficult it is to acquire or maintain the habit of mind he would urge on his readers.

His sharing of the various escape temptations is illustrated in an early poem, "Arrival," and in rather recent one, "Forget What Did." In the first he finds himself in a new city. Since the prospect of a totally new beginning momentarily fascinates him, he celebrates his anonymity in new surroundings:

Now let me lie down, under
A wide-branched indifference,

. . . .

For this ignorance of me
Seems a kind of innocence.

Though immediately aware that his own past will soon "impound" the "milk-aired Eden" of such innocence, he hopes, nonetheless, to hang on to this euphoric feeling. Of course, his recollection of its transiency signals the start of its demise.

In "Forget What Did," written perhaps twenty years later, we find him still trying to forget his past and the identity it suggests, this time by stopping his diary entries. Rather than continuing to be "cicatrized" "By such words, such actions / As bleakened waking," he determines that the empty pages, if ever filled will record "Celestial recurrences, / The day the flowers come, / And when the birds go." Though failing to reverse the escapist direction of his thinking, he vows only to record things selectively, not to experience them in this fashion. As in "For Sidney Bechet," where he relishes escaping to the "Crescent City" evoked by old jazz records, and in "The Importance of Elsewhere," where he recognizes his need to get away from himself, Larkin in this poem decides to create in his diary a romantic past to which he can occasionally repair. The tension between reality and dream forces him to this expediency.

Poems like "Forget What Did" support the view of one critic that for Larkin an important way of maintaining equilibrium in a stressful existence is occasional engagement with the past; for him the past can operate as a means of liberation form the tedious present.[21] Most of his poems support, too, the contention that though Larkin's treatment of the world is essentially an unillusioned dismissal, this dismissal is a "proud, self-affirming act." Larkin's popularity has been traced to his finding poetry and humor in sterile reality and thus making it bearable for his readers: "He shows that it can be borne with grace and gentleness."[22]

Gentleness certainly characterizes his treatment of people, as well as circumstances. The call for clear vision and honesty in most of his poems, coupled with his understanding of how easily one can look at things with less than clear vision, prompts him frequently to respond with feeling for those caught in the pull between unpleasant reality and desired romance. Sympathy, as a byproduct of honest self-appraisal, thus becomes a central habit of mind for Larkin. The detail with which he sketches his characters and contemporary England, rather than suggesting contempt for them or their world, reflects a quiet caring. We have seen him implicitly advocating such an attitude by his expressed concern for a rapist and religion of a century ago, without condoning rape or superstition.

But, If Larkin's brand of honesty or clear vision is always tinged with sympathetic regret that things must be as they are, his sympathy refuses to be sentimental. Thus "The Dedicated " shows his insight into the selfless withdrawal of those individuals given to quiet service:

> Some must employ the scythe
> Upon the grasses,
> That the walks be smooth
> For the feet of the angel.

While mindful of their dedication, their sincerity, and the modesty of their desires—"contentment / If the feet of the dove / Perch on the scythe's handle, / perch once, and then depart / Their knowledge"—he nowhere subscribes himself to their type or degree of dedication, nor does he fail to remind us, in the final lines, of the harsh outcome of their vocation:

> After, they wait
> Only the colder advent,
> The quenching of candles.

This realistic sympathy appears in two other very short poems: "Wants," where Larkin grimly but feelingly characterizes our desire beyond superficial social obligations as a wish to be alone, and that behind our seeming aversion to death as the desire for the oblivion which death seems to promise; and "Wires," where he implicitly compares our painful but necessary growing up through disappointed idealism to cattle's learning the perimeters defined by electric fences.

Similarly, "Nothing To Be Said" suggests that despite the conservatism of Larkin's outlook, he retains a perhaps more genuine feeling for the common man than many professing more liberal political views, as he observes:

> For nations vague as weed,
> For nomads among stones,

> Small-statured cross-faced tribes
> And cobble-close families
> In mill-towns on dark mornings
> Life is slow dying.

This loving attitude points to perhaps the ultimate value behind Larkin's poems. For all of the unsentimental qualities of his style and viewpoint, he offers human affection as the one ideal worth the risk attendant upon all idealizing. Even if love itself is largely an illusion, likely to disappoint, Larkin is unable to blame his characters for following it to its usually unrewarding conclusion. This is one reason why he intends us not to disapprove of the implied decision by the distraught lover in "If, My Darling" to keep his true nature a secret from his girl friend; his opting for a loving relationship, even at the price of some deceit, appears prudent.

The frequency of the outsider as a character in Larkin's poetry has been noted. While the outsider's position affords the best opportunity for the unsentimental honesty and sympathy approved by Larkin, by a cruel irony it tends to keep the outsider from the ultimate in attainable human happiness. The most honest and sympathetic figures in Larkin's world go largely unrewarded; with rare exception those habits of mind become merely their own rewards, necessary but insufficient for genuine joy. The outsider for Larkin is always a pathetic figure.

Of course, the pathos of the outsider lacking in awareness or feeling is readily apparent. The subject of most rationalization in Larkin's poetry is the failure to enjoy love. The various rationalizers, such as the speakers in "Self's the Man" and "Dockery and Son," betray, by their very attempt at self-justification, the desperation of their positions. No less powerfully Larkin presents in "Mr. Bleaney" a speaker intent on scorning Bleaney and his way of living. As the poem develops we learn that, despite the shabbiness of his surroundings, Bleaney loved and was loved. The landlady speaks of how he took her small garden "Properly in hand." Her telling the speaker of "The Frinton folk / Who put him up for summer holidays, / And Christmas at his sister's house in Stoke" suggests that for Bleaney these were more than superficial relationships. Judging from his treatment of the landlady and her respectful remembrance of him, Bleaney probably mattered as much to these other people as they mattered to him. By the end of the poem the speaker recognizes, that, despite the superiority he would assume toward Bleaney, he occupies the same shabby room but without those loving relationships which helped redeem Bleaney's life. He cannot know even that Bleaney shared the self-doubt and dread of dying which he clearly feels. His stuffing his ears with cotton "to drown / The jabbering set he egged her on to buy" appears in retrospect a futile attempt to drown out his rising feeling that the love given and received by Bleaney defines the crucial difference between them.

Three poems illustrate in more positive fashion the value Larkin attaches to human affection., He has described "Broadcast" as "about as near as I get in this collection [The Whitsun Weddings] to a lovesong (It's not, I'm afraid, very near)."[23] Certainly it is the only of his poems showing a lover totally unthreatened in his love. In the poem love takes the form of the speaker, as he listens to a Sunday concert over the BBC, which his beloved is attending, trying to see her in his mind. Anxious to pick her out of the crowd and not to lose her once she is captured in his imagination, he exhibits sensitivity to the details of her dress and sympathy for its necessary dowdiness. While his vision becomes distorted, first by the music and then by its sudden cessation, we see him nevertheless wholly absorbed in loving devotion. The poem seems to stress more the self-consuming power of that devotion than its futility.

"The Whitsun Weddings" illustrates what Larkin might see as a rarer kind of love, in that it combines generous affection with objective insight. The poem turns on the narrator-protagonist's realization of having intimately shared an experience with people toward whom he initially felt indifference. We have here the typical Larkin loner, unmarried and apparently middle-aged, only gradually noticing the many newlyweds joining him on the train as he journeys to London. With increasing detail he chronicles the appearance and behavior of the wedding parties gathered in stations along the way. Combining humor with sympathy, his observations culminate in his wonder at having been thrown in with them. Though alone in his meditations—"none / Thought of the others they would never meet / Or how their lives would all contain this hour"—he manages to share, in his own way, their sense of momentous personal change. Just as marriage has joined two formerly separate lives, chance has married his life to theirs.

Like the speaker in "Church Going," the narrator here respects such joinings. He is awed by "this frail/ Travelling coincidence" and the sense of destiny it inspires: "What it held / Stood ready to be loosed with all the power / That being changed can give." At the end of the journey he feels a sense of separating—"A sense of falling, like an arrow-shower / Sent out of sight, somewhere becoming rain"—but, as these images suggest, also a sense of an almost miraculous fertilization. In this poem we see a man roused to affection for the variety of folk who have traveled with him, struck by the happy fortuitousness of the event into a love for them which will continue. The narrative itself evidences such continuation. Larkin shows the fruit of affection even when it is wholly internalized and unreciprocated. While suggesting that the wedding parties, as well as the traveler hmself, have been caught up in a seemingly predestined pattern, he gives this fatalism a happy reading. The key to such happiness is the affection which he summons to the occasion. By it the outsider transforms himself into an insider.

This ideal of a realizable love is the subject of another equally moving poem, "An Arundel Tomb," where Larkin meditates on the stone effigies of an earl and a countess in Chichester Cathedral. Passing over various details of the tomb, he notices, "with a sharp tender shock," that their hands are joined. This he finds a curious detail, potentially insignificant against the elaborate decoration of the tomb. Yet, he is struck by the fact that this is the one detail that he, a modern observer, sees as neither dated nor ridiculous. Presumably intended to maintain the respect given the earl and countess in life, the heavily stylized effigies have come to mean less and less to passersby in succeeding centuries:

> Now, helpless in the hollow of
> An unarmorial age, a trough
> Of smoke in slow suspended skeins
> Above their scrap of history,
> Only an attitude remains.

The irony of his noticing what may have been but a gesture to love suggests to Larkin the greater irony, that time sorts out our gestures toward immortality and ultimately respects those corresponding most closely to genuine human feelings and needs. While what the medieval couple thought would immortalize them has gone largely unnoticed, "The stone fidelity/ They hardly meant has come to be/ Their final blazon." Because for Larkin love constitutes man's supreme attempt to declare the importance of a human life, and to ward off the insecurity and impermanence inherent in our existence, the finally human detail of the locked hands—despite its original insignificance for the sculptor and his patrons—moves him

to realize the force of that ideal. "What will survive of us is love,"
he concludes.

This preeminence of love in Larkin's scheme of values might
seem surprising. Certainly it connects him with that romantic view
of life intent upon disparaging. However, compared with those
earlier twentieth-century poets—especially Yeats, Auden, and
Thomas—who sustained that view in various versions, Larkin
appears much more determined to depict love as a largely unat-
tainable goal. He depicts the consequences of failed love not as a
potentially glamorous Byronic despair, but simply as an unexciting
descent back into the dull existence making up most of life. His
repeated insistence that common sense need not preclude feeling
and affection, indeed that it must not, makes him no more a sen-
timentalist than Swift or Pope, and probably constitutes a major
source of the humane appeal his poems have had.

CHAPTER 4

Structure and Order

O NE quality which both admirers and detractors of Philip Larkin have noticed is the sense of order which almost every one of his poems creates. Although many of his poems have aroused interpretive disputes and disagreement over precisely what happens in them or what is completed by their endings, each gives the impression that something indeed has been completed. As much as more specific technical elements or the operative assumptions of his poems, this sense of form has caused critics to link Larkin with the Augustan tradition in English verse.[1] And, along with diction and syntax, this ready sense of structure has lured many readers into regarding his poetry as easily understood. As with Yeats or Auden, they are frequently surprised by disarmingly subtle implications in poems of seeming simplicity.

If form is readily intuited in Larkin's poems, it is not always so easily pinned down. Like most other poets, Larkin presents poems held together either by actions of some moral or emotional quality, by fairly tight arguments, or by rhetorical statements. Of course, action, logic, and rhetoric operate simultaneously in most of the poems. To say that a particular poem is held together by any one is only to identify its ultimate emphasis.

I *Poems of Action*

Some recurring types of action in the poems have already been mentioned. Perhaps foremost of these, and one often said to reveal most sharply the peculiar issues and values of Larkin's world-view, is rationalization: a number of his most effective poems involve attempts somehow to justify unsatisfactory states of affairs. Some of these attempts—notably "Toads," "Toads Revisited," and "Poetry of Departures"—prove successful, at least from the speaker's point of view. The implication in each of these poems is that he doesn't

mind all that much being stuck, so that his gestures of rebellion are
no more than gestures. The ease with which he talks himself out of
breaking away suggests that he is less rebellious or dissatisfied than
he would like to think. The amusement generated by these poems
depends on the combination of self-delusion and likeable personality. Because Larkin carefully depicts his speakers in these three
poems as witty, we can enjoy their expressions of disatisfaction, but
because he exposes them as rationalizers—would-be doubters blind-
ed by egoism and the limitations of their wit—we need not take
their ultimate relapse into work or routine very seriously.

Other poems showing rationalization prove much less amusing.
One difference is in the personal issue the character debates with
himself: where in the two "Toads" poems and "Poetry of Departures" the speakers weigh the merits of work and routine against the
lure of idleness and escape, in these others they consider the much
more depressing and seemingly inescapable dilemma of loneliness
and increasing age. Each finds himself trying to justify a situation
ultimately unjustifiable. Its unjustifiability he recognizes by the end
of the poem, since, unlike the ultimately content rationalizers, he
cannot blind himself to the truth of his situation. These poems thus
depict sadly unsuccessful, rather than amusingly successful,
attempts at self-justification. The bachelor in "Self's the Man,"
having shown that his bachelorhood is no more selfish a choice than
his friend Arnold's married state, feels compelled to go beyond
moral self-justification by proving himself the happier man. This
compulsion leads him to admit, in the last line, that Arnold may be
the happier and that, despite his freedom from a nagging wife,
noisy children, and a mother-in-law, he may be closer to madness.
The unifying action of the poem is this discovery, which makes him
fully aware of why he first felt it necessary to compare himself with
Arnold, and overthrows by forceful contrast the light tone with
which he disparaged Arnold's situation up the final stanza.

Similar reversals, whereby the speaker almost succeeds in justify-
ing himself only to suffer a disheartening realization of the emptiness of his situation, occur in "Reasons for Attendance" and "Mr.
Bleaney." While self-discovery and self-revelation run throughout
the one speaker's argument favoring isolation, the roomer in "Mr.
Bleaney" reveals and discovers himself only in his final sentence. In
each case the resources of rationalization give way to honesty, sensitivity, and unhappiness, to produce a sharp, sad conclusion.

"Dockery and Son" represents a more complex instance of discovery following rationalization. The occasion is a man's return to his old college after some twenty years. Though his reasons for returning are not given, his visiting with his old Dean, trying the door of his old rooms, recognizing the chime of a "known bell," and noting how people generally ignore him suggest some desire to renew the sense of belonging which he associates with his college days. His description of himself in the Dean's office as "death-suited," and the lines "I try the door of where I used to live: / Locked" signify an attempt to leave a dead present for a past in which he believes he was truly alive. To him, therefore, the most disturbing remnant of his wasted visit to the college turns out to be the news that Dockery, a former classmate, has a son now in college; this provides the impetus for the gloomy remainder of the poem. He is struck not so much that a contemporary should be married and have a son—this he has already learned to deal with—as by Dockery's son being so old. Even before his intense meditation on this phenomenon, Larkin has him notice the rail lines, "Joining and parting," and the "strong/ Unhindered moon" which they reflect. For the speaker these operate as reminders of the riddle he is to solve: how far Dockery's path has diverged from his, how much clearer Dockery's foresight must have been, and how much time has gone out of his life. Once this challenge to his self-esteem is fully upon him, he proceeds to scrutinize Dockery's presumed motives, the assumptions behind them, and the legitimacy of such assumptions in explaining what happens to people.

Specifically, he first attributes to Dockery the ability to take stock of what he wanted, but rejects this as not really explaining the difference between them. He next shifts to the explanation that Dockery was "[C]onvinced . . . he should be added to"—a highly speculative assumption, given the vagaries of procreation and childbirth—and goes on to attack as questionable the notion that adding means increase. "To me it was dilution," he insists, as he finds all such "innate assumptions" divorced from the truth of our lives. All of this rather pathetic examination derives from his Dean's chance mention of a man whom he can scarcely remember and about whom he knows almost nothing. His persistence in building a line of reasoning on so shallow a foundation of fact suggests a desperate self-defensiveness, which, at least prior to the poem's beginning, he has been able to contain. The news of Dockery has broken those thin defenses and exposed him once more to the grim truth of his prospects. Now, unable to assert that, in rugged defiance of people like Dockery, he pursued "undilution," he finds inexplicable not only what happened to Dockery—whatever that was—but what has happened to himself. The mental bout with Dockery has momentarily diverted him from the underlying awareness that, for reasons he cannot know, he has nothing to show for his time.

Unlike the speakers in many Hardy poems, Larkin's aging bachelor cannot even believe in a chance-filled universe; he feels entirely ignorant. Assumptions like "increase" or "dilution" represent for him a "style / Our lives bring with them: habit for a while, / Suddenly they harden into all we've got." His use of plural pronouns in these lines signals his realization that, whatever Dockery's motives, such assumptions have informed his own view of others, himself, and the divergences of life. Yet, he must admit that he cannot improve on them. Loneliness and ignorance together prove inescapably disheartening:

> Life is first boredom, then fear.
> Whether or not we use it, it goes,
> And leaves what something hidden from us chose,
> And age, and then the only end of age.

Partly because he cannot explain away an understandably painful situation, we sympathize with him much more than with those who can.

Other Larkin poems center on disheartening discoveries without attempted rationalization. In "Lines on a Young Lady's Photograph Album" the man examining the snapshots from his girl friend's past moves from an intimation of the precariousness of their relationship to an admission that it is ended. The photo album itself serves as catalyst for this discovery. After expressing joy at her permitting him to examine the album, he begins a series of meditations on the pictures and the excitement they bring, which forces him to admit that with that concession she has abandoned him. He feels his self-control repeatedly assaulted by her beauty, by boyfriends of the past, and by the artificiality of looking at old pictures of someone alive and nearby. Concerned with the need to preserve their relationship, he questions the efficacy of memory and its highly selective surrogate, photography. He wonders whether a photograph can preserve a sufficiently real likeness while particulars are being dispersed in ordinary time. Later in the poem he even questions whether his nostalgia for her past may not be a cover for the lack of genuine emotion. Implicit in his growing skepticism is doubt about the quality of his love, and about what the girl means to him: an image, a fact, a memory, past, present, or what. He cannot tell, but he can recognize that his being relegated to such meditation itself indicates an irreparable loss. In the end he finds himself mourning her, sadly resigned to stealing her photo: "to condense . . . a past that no one now can share, / No matter whose your future." Conceding his loss of her now and in the future, he offers a pathetic paeon to the snapshot: "calm and dry / It holds you like a heaven, and you lie / Unvariably lovely there, / Smaller and clearer as the years go by." "Smaller and clearer," and less his, as he wearily tries to extract some satisfaction from what he has seen to be a most unsatisfactory loss. Though weak in character, he exhibits a common weakness; his sad realization and the humiliating terms on which it occurs seem pitiable.

Less pathetic but no less sad is the main action of "Money." Its character, probably older than the man in "Lines . . .," begins by imagining his money reproaching him: "Why do you let me lie here wastefully? / I am all you never had of goods and sex. / You could still get them by writing a few cheques." After comparing his unpropertied state with the houses, cars, and wives of other men, he concludes that "money has something to do with life." At this point he takes off from the conclusion in an unexpected way. In his opening remarks the question has been whether he should spend his money for some of the real living he has missed; the implication of the imagined reproach, his survey of others, and the conclusion he draws seems to be that he should. But now, in a manner suggestive of his shrewdness, he shifts the issue to whether he can buy happiness anymore. Remembering that "You can't put off being young until you retire," he realizes, by analogy, that time has diluted the power of his money to make him happy, partly by economic inflation but mostly by making him older and less capable of enjoying the good things of life: "[H]owever you bank your screw, the money you save / Won't in the end buy you more than a shave." The connection between money and life proves cruelly intimate. Because he engages in none of the excuse-making or sour-grapes reasoning of Larkin's various rationalizers, he commands admiration as well as sympathy.

The speakers in "Money" and "Lines . . ." both consider general questions about existence arising out of personal dissatisfaction. The answers they find compound that dissatisfaction. Sometimes Larkin writes poems structured by characters examining some aspect of their behavior. The results may be satisfying or unsatisfying. Such a poem is "Vers de Société," where the speaker learns the real reason he would choose to waste his time at a cocktail party. A happier discovery is made by the young man in "Church Going," who ponders the implications of his often visiting country churches despite his disbelief in the dogma associated with them. Each character questions his attachment to a convention to which he feels superior. For the partygoer this produces the realization that, like most people his age, he prefers dull socializing to frightening solitude, because the latter reminds him of failure and approaching death. "Only the young can be alone freely," he concludes. Likewise Larkin's churchgoer finds a commonsense reason for his attraction to the church: the metaphysical hungerings which he shares with most men.

Each character reaches his conclusions through a progressive thought pattern. The steady way in which each works toward a solution of his particular puzzle, as well as the way in which the steps and the solution are couched, suggest forthrightness and humaneness. The man in "Vers de Société" is middle-aged and lonely. After parodying the style of an invitation he has received and after considering refusal, he is struck by his disinclination to be alone any evening:

> Just think of all the spare time that has flown
>
> Straight into nothingness by being filled
> With forks and faces, rather than repaid
> Under a lamp, hearing the noise of wind,
> And looking out to see the moon thinned
> To an air-sharpened blade.

This image recalls the moon in "Dockery and Son." And, as in the earlier poem, the speaker follows his remarks on the moon with an examination of commonly held assumptions, in this case the notion that solitude is selfish and virtue social: "[T]he big wish / Is to have people nice to you, which means / Doing it back somehow," he declares. But is such behavior very nice or very unselfish?: "Are then these routines / Playing at goodness, like going to church?" He rejects the idea of partygoing as either a wholly superficial gesture at kindness or a futile attempt at goodness. Instead he decides that for him the party holds an attraction at once more selfish and more profound: it temporarily relieves him of the remorse for lack of accomplishment and life's brevity which would plague him were he alone. If not a pleasant conclusion, this at least seems a reasonable one; it offers assurance that his partygoing is neither capricious nor insincere. Because he now knows that life makes him desperate to attend, the poem ends with his accepting the invitation.

"Church Going" proceeds in an equally persistent manner, revealing the seriousness and the sincerity of its character. In the opening stanzas he recounts his most recent visit to a church. He vacillates between respect and annoyance. After taking off his cycle-clips "in awkward reference" and carefully noting the details and arrangement of the interior, he feels obligated to undo the piety of such behavior with a mocking pronouncement from the lectern. Upon leaving, he signs the book and donates a small coin, while thinking that he should not have stopped. Yet, realizing that he often stops at such places, he begins to explore the puzzle of his behavior by speculating on what will happen to churches once they become entirely unused. He considers the possibilities of a few cathedrals remaining as museum-pieces, of churches' being avoided out of dread, and of their attracting superstitious cure-seekers. Speculating on the identity of the very last visitor, who he imagines will be someone like himself, he attributes to the church an attractiveness profounder than that drawing the "ruin-bibber" or "Christmas-addict," derisive terms which foreshadow his embrace of profounder motives as his own.

Having separated himself initially from orthodox believers and, as the poem has progressed, from superficial attenders and non-believers, he is forced to concede not only that somebody like himself would probably be the last churchgoer, but that such churchgoing will never cease. Because the church is a "serious house . . . [i]n whose blent air all our compulsions meet, / Are recognized, and robed as destinies," and because secularization has separated and diluted those compulsions, he can only conclude that "someone will forever be surprising / A hunger in himself to be more serious, / And gravitating to this ground." This conclusion confirms him in the reasonableness of his own churchgoing by suggesting that he is neither alone nor inconsistent in his behavior. Because he is honest and searching, the reader can respect him and be pleased that he has resolved his puzzle.

"I Remember, I Remember" offers a most interesting variation of this pattern of puzzled self-examination. There Larkin's character confronts his inability to recall his childhood. The occasion is a train trip with a friend taking him through Coventry, his birthplace, which he has not seen for many years. Stopping in the station, he delightedly looks out the window for remembered landmarks, only to discover that nothing looks familiar. The balance of the poem consists of the friend's asking him if he has his "roots" in Coventry, his imagined sarcastic reply, and a final exchange between them.

From the poem's beginning he evinces a desperate need for a sense of belonging somewhere. Though not alone, he feels up-rooted, and views Coventry as a happy opportunity for fixing himself in place and time. The unfamiliarity of what he sees there causes him to feel that Coventry is "where my childhood was un-spent" and to construct in his mind a map of places where nothing noteworthy happened to him. Wittily inverting the clichés of romantic poetry, he speaks of

> Our garden . . . where I did not invent
> Blinding theologies of flowers and fruits . . .
> The bracken where I never trembling sat,

> Determined to go through with it; where she
> Lay back and "all became a burning mist."
> . . . those offices [where] my dogerrel
> Was not set up in blunt ten-point, nor read
> By a distinguished cousin of the mayor,
> Who didn't call and tell my father *There*
> *Before us, had we the gift to see ahead*—

The sustained allusions to a poem by Thomas Hood of the same title and a similar poem by Praed have been noted.[2] Though Larkin clearly means to undercut romantic assumptions about childhood and the poetry inspired by them, his way of doing so suggests that while he may not admire such poems or such assumptions, he does take them seriously. If the main character's account of his non-childhood represents an amusing satire on the Hood poem and others like it, in context it expresses his bitter regret that for all he can verify he did not exist during those earlier years. His disorientation resembles that of John Kemp, the antihero of *Jill*, who visits his home town immediately after a wartime bombing raid has largely destroyed it. Mistakenly expecting to recall his past, as a corrective to his unexciting present, the character in the poem overreacts in his derisive chart of his childhood by alluding to a type of upbringing in which he could never believe. But, as one critic has noted, the poem operates as "disguised regret": if not sorry he did not have the stock romantic childhood, he never abandons his wish that childhood had been something more than it was.[3] His calmer realization in the end that, "[I]t's not the place's fault . . . Nothing, like something, happens anywhere," reveals disillusionment not only with his life, which seemingly has given him little to remember, but with himself for momentarily succumbing to the alluring possibility of such recollections. He realizes that by his bitter account he has exaggerated his wishes and thus distorted his problem. Though profiting by his discovery—he will not so easily fall prey to the romantic illusion of childhood again—he seems no happier for it.

In this regard "The Whitsun Weddings," another of Larkin's discovery poems, is a striking exception. There the speaker develops a totally satisfying insight into his situation. Where the shallowness of modern life defines whatever comfort Larkin's churchgoer derives from his realizations, it is completely forgotten in "The Whitsun Weddings," so much so that the poem has been cited as perhaps indicative of a change in Larkin's viewpoint.[4] It is notable among Larkin's poems, too, for describing a wholly fortituous happy discovery.

More often, of course, Larkin's people have to search for their satisfactions. Emotional shifts, whether positive or negative, rarely develop by themselves. Those poems showing such shifts illustrate the studied behavior of most of his speakers. "For Sidney Bechet" shows the Larkin character listening to a jazz record and moving to a climax of ecstatic pleasure: "Oh, play that thing! . . . On me your voice falls as they say love should, / Like an enormous yes." Contrasting the "Crescent City" of his stirred imagination with fluctuating, imperfect reality, he praises the "speech" of the saxophone improvisations as the "natural noise of good, / Scattering long-haired grief and scored pity." If the pleasure from such listening is only temporary, it is temporily real, and the result of a deliberate move. If dependent upon the jazzman's artistry, he nevertheless helps produce his own triumph over "long-haired grief and scored pity."

"Reference Back" finds the jazz enthusiast not so successful in his escape attempt. The difference seems to be that here he listens to

jazz during a visit home. His mother depresses him by responding
to a classic blues rendering with what he regards as a banal comment, "That was a pretty one." Rather than escaping a time-filled
world through jazz, he is reminded of it all the more. He merely
reiterates what he has known and had hoped to forget temporarily,
that "Truly, though our element is time, / We are not suited to the
long perspectives / Open at each instant of our lives." He fears that
he will always connect King Oliver's *Riverside Blues* with his
mother's remarks and that, instead of bringing him much-needed
respite, the music will forever remind him of the futility of bridging
any gap in time or of going home in any meaningful sense.

"Absences" shows different responses to a different stimulus.
There the speaker enjoys an ecstasy of imagination as he envisions,
first, the sea, "that tilts and sighs," and then moves in to an even
freer dimension, the sky. The freely ranging imagination in the
poem, the final exclamations—"Such attics cleared of me! Such
absences!"—and Larkin's comment that he likes the subject of the
poem because he is "always thrilled by the thought of what places
look like when I am not there"[5]—suggest the likelihood of a *tour de
force*. That the excitement of the speaker is self-induced, wholly
through the power of his imagination, and without any external
stimulus, makes this especially notable among Larkin's lyrics.

All of the poems discussed thus far in terms of their unifying actions display shifts—in attitude, in understanding, or in action—by
their central characters or speakers. All of the various people of
those poems undergo changes which will have some permanent
bearing. A much greater proportion of Larkin's poems feature
speech or thought indicative not of change but of that which will
not change—a character, a state of mind, a feeling, or a situation.
The pattern of such poems is circular rather than progressive.

One group of such poems are those involving successful
rationalization, where the speaker backs off from a possible shift in
his attitude and reverts to what he has been before. In "Toads" and
"Toads Revisited" we find the same person trying to reconcile his
attachment to his job with his basic dislike of work. The question
facing him at the beginning of each is why, if he dislikes his job, he
doesn't get out of it. His attempts to answer that question prove
amusingly evasive.

In the earlier poem he begins by asking why he should surrender
to work: "Can't I use my wit as a pitchfork/ And drive the brute
off?" he asks. "Wit" is the key to his subsequent reasoning, as he

cites numerous types of people surviving by their wits: "Lecturers, lispers, / Losels, loblolly men, louts." The increasingly disparaging terms of this list foreshadow his ultimate rejection of unemployment. Having wished for the courage to swear off job security and his pension, he recognizes something "toad-like" in his character—perhaps a conditioned commitment to the work-ethic—which prevents such escape. Yet, he abandons the objectivity of this self-appraisal by remarking that the toad within will not permit him to "blarney" his way to "fame and the girl and money." "Blarney" signifies a moralistic judgment of those whom he began his poem envying, as well as the inevitability of his remaining with his job. His final statement—that while work may embody morality, "It's hard to lose either, / When you have both"—contains for him a reason for not quitting and for the reader a mark of his cowardice.

The similarly titled sequel follows a more pragmatic but no less specious line of reasoning. The initial admission that "Walking around in the park / Should feel better than work" suggests dissatisfaction similar to that prompting the earlier poem. Here the ultimate rationale for work is the obvious and largely irrelevant argument that working is preferable to the empty lives of the sick and seedy frequenters of the park. If this argument denotes an older speaker than in the other Toads poem, it denotes, too, a greater refusal to face the real issue. Even more than before he comes off as self-deluding and evasive. Similar question-begging occurs in "Poetry of Departures," where, having denounced the ordinary dullness of his life's routine, the speaker says he would throw up everything if to do so didn't seem so artificial and deliberate.

A more ccomplex brand of rationalization occurs in "Latest Face." Its occasion is the speaker's spotting a pretty girl. His labeling her face the "latest" suggests that there have been many others and probably will be many more, and that his response is more or less typical for him. In an amusing departure from the ordinary boy-meets-girl pattern, Larkin has him ultimately dodge the "latest face," to betray a basic weakness. Addressing the girl in his mind, he first asks for some sort of psychic recognition of his attention to her beauty, but then plunges into a semiphilosophical explanation of why they cannot know happiness together, which verges on rationalization for his own indecisiveness. He confirms his decision not to pursue her further by wondering, very abstrusely, whether she really would prefer concrete action to his distant worship, as the real relationship might well destroy her power over him. Though concluding with this question, his failure to answer implies a decision not to act. Though wanting to know and love the girl, he cannot command sufficient courage to act. Instead, in a habitual ploy, he appropriates philosophical principles to justify not doing so. His decision, while perhaps as certain as those of the other rationalizers, seems not so satisfactory to him, as if he suspects he has trapped himself. The greater seriousness of his problem and of the poem's tone makes him more pathetic than the others.

Another small group of poems feature characters reverting to what they have been or have felt, but without rationalization. The speaker in "High Windows" recounts an experience which occurs whenever he sees "a couple of kids / And guess he's fucking her and she's / Taking pills or wearing a diaphragm." His immediate response is that

> . . . this is paradise
>
> Everyone old has dreamed of all their lives—
> Bonds and gestures pushed to one side
> Like an outdated combine harvester. . . .

But then, he associates this response with what he imagins to have been the similar response of an older person forty years back to his generation's apparent liberation from religious difficulties—"*That'll be the life; / No God any more*"—and experiences a sharp turn of mind:

> Rather than words comes the thought of high windows:
> The sun-comprehending glass,
> And beyond it, the deep blue air, that shows
> Nothing, and is nowhere, and is endless.

Just as the twentieth century's removal of God has not relieved man of what Larkin elsewhere terms a "hunger in himself to be more serious" ("Church Going"), the puzzles of sexuality and love have not been solved by proclaiming a sexual revolution. Because he is middle-aged and presumably unmarried, and because he has grown up in an era of greater sexual restriction, the speaker's momentary envy of the young people is understandable. But, his sense of justice keeps him from envying them very long. Rather than learning something new, we see him forgetting and then quickly recalling something already assimilated into his view of life.

While he probably will forget again, perhaps the next time he sees a "couple of kids," the poem illustrates the judgment which will rescue him from such a reflexive error.

Not so positive but equally circular is "Sad Steps." There Larkin is startled by the moon, "High and preposterous and separate." He considers various interpretations—"Lozenge of love! Medallion of art! / O wolves of memory! Immensements!"—all of which yield to his decision that

> The hardness and brightness and the plain
> Far-reaching singleness of that wide stare
> Is a reminder of the strength and pain
> Of being young; that it can't come again,
> But is for others undiminished somewhere.

Larkin here orders his materials so that only at the end do we see why he was so taken by the moon. Given his usual preoccupations with time's passing and lost youth, which remain strong even after he has ceased looking out his window, he probably will be similarly seduced by the moon on many clear nights to come.

All of the poems structured by circular behavior depend on the possibility of change, albeit an unrealized possibility. Many others involve more static forms. Not only does the character not change, but the question of his changing is made to seem largely irrelevant. A good example of such structuring is "If, My Darling," where by his amusing self-doubt, his wit, his honesty, and his implicit decision to stay as he is, the young man wins our approval. Conversely, the lover in "Maiden Name" exhibits a pathetic spitefulness when he muses on the maiden name of a former girl friend now married. His remarks suggest a penchant for philosophy: he considers the significance of the girl's name, what happens to it when she marries, and what it means now. However, his praise of her youthful beauty and of her maiden name as a means of preserving the memory of that beauty reveals a pervasive bitterness. Attempting to conceal his disappointment, he insults what is by flattering what was. Even more than the stolen snapshot in "Lines on a Young Lady's Photograph Album," the maiden name appears a ridiculous, even pathetic means of alleviating that disappointment.

A more positive approach to love and the setbacks time inevitably brings the lover is found in "Love Songs in Age," where a widow comes upon popular sheet music collected in her youth. Forced by the old tunes and lyrics to reconsider "that much-mentioned

brilliance, love"—"Its bright incipience sailing above, / Still
promising to solve, and satisfy, / And set unchangeably in
order"—she is forced by her mature vision to recognize that "To
pile them back, to cry, / Was hard, without lamely admitting
how / It had not done so then, and could not now." She knows
better than when she was young, and she knows that she knows
better. Finding the music by accident, she resists its false promise
by the force of her character.

Another instance of character triumphing over adversity occurs in
"Skin," where the speaker reacts to age not with the melancholy of
most Larkin characters, but with witty remarks to his "Obedient
daily dress." Acknowledging the faithful service of his skin, which
has learned its "lines" well, he ends by apologizing that when
young he found no suitable occasion on which to wear it. With
mature vision comparable to that of the widow playing her old
songs, he reveals characteristic resources of wit by which he avoids
the terrible gloom others might read into his situation. Diverting
our attention from such gloom, he seems to divert himself, as well.

A larger group of static poems point more to situation than to
character. The situation may be of varying specificity. The happy
circumstances of the devoted lover in "Broadcast" and of the
reformed diary-writer of "Forget What Did" have been described.
Each reflects the security of wise or fortunate choices. A situation
stemming from a less fortunate choice is shown in "Wild Oats,"
where the protagonist amusingly regrets having pursued the
homelier "friend in specs" instead of "bosomy English rose." The
speaker in "The Importance of Elsewhere" suffers an equally unfortunate plight. Having been away for some time, he confesses that
home prohibits him from feeling other than out of place; he cannot
escape his oddness.

Still another kind of discomfort is shown in the seventh selection
of *XX Poems* ("Since the majority of me") and "No Road"; in each
the speaker has second thoughts about having terminated a
friendship. With appropriate metaphors each reveals his internal
conflict between pride and regret. One speaks of the "majority" of
himself and of the other person having agreed to part, but notes
wistfully a silent minority, at least within himself, which yet
questions the decision:

> A silence of minorities
> That, unopposed at last, returns

> Each night with cancelled promises
> They want renewed. They never learn.

His dilemma is compounded in "No Road," where the speaker envisions the road connecting him with his former friend eventually giving way to a world where no such road will run. The prospect of watching such a world arise disturbs him: "Not to prevent it is my will's fulfillment. / Willing it, my ailment." The freedom he sought now seems only a negative gain. Having felt locked into the relationship, he now fears being permanently locked out. But, despite his awareness no relief from the stalemate is suggested. Presumably time will destroy whatever connectives have remained.

Where these characters are unhappy because of the certainty of their situations, in at least two Larkin poems characters are troubled by uncertainty. In one, "Wedding Winds," we find a young bride the day after her wedding-night suffering a sense of foreboding. Having experienced timeless bliss the night before and having wondered that any creature should lack her joy, she now finds herself totally in time. Though finding no immediate reason for unhappiness, she intuits the erosion of happiness. The poem shows an intensification of her foreboding, the ultimate object of which is death.

In the other poem, originally included in *XX Poems* and later added to the revised edition of *The North Ship* ("Waiting for breakfast, while she brushed her hair"), the speaker, also on a cold morning after, has found himself suddenly able to create images in a way he has been unable to for some time. The "featureless morning," which by his description of the cobblestone and mist seems just that, now takes on a much more exciting cast:

> Misjudgment: for the stones slept, and the mist
> Wandered absolvingly past all it touched,
> Yet hung like a stayed breath; the lights burnt on,
> Pin-points of undisturbed excitement. . . .

Having regained the "lost world" of his imagination, he wonders whether pursuit of his art will require giving up the girl he loves. In the final lines he asks his muse:

> Are you jealous of her?
> Will you refuse to come till I have sent
> Her terribly away, importantly live.
> Part invalid, part baby, and part saint?

These situations are all fairly specific. A number of poems show situations more general but in some ways more personal. A miniature spectrum of psychological sets is contained in the three poems dealing with the approach of spring. Significantly Larkin writes of no very positive response. The guardedly hopeful attitude of the speaker in "Coming," who feels himself mysteriously inspired and "starts to be happy," is as close as Larkin comes. The virtual distrust of spring's message expressed by the persona in "The Trees" has been noted; it signals a gloomier state of mind. And, in "Spring," we see a man able to accept that message for others, yet sadly unable to respond to it himself. An unnamed grief prevents a total response in each poem and provokes varying degrees of sympathy for each speaker.

Still other poems suggest, in general terms, their characters' regret upon looking back on life. The paradoxical trap of perspective which prohibits proximity is movingly described in "Age," as is that of the bachelor in "Places, Loved Ones," who feels bound by the public stereotype of carefree bachelorhood to continue playing that role despite his loneliness. Equally regretful are the altruist of "Sympathy in White Major" as he wearily recalls a lifetime of service to others, and the speaker in "How Distant" as he notes the gap separating him from youthful setting forth. In all of these poems we are asked to respond to the ongoing emotional crises of people as they move through middle age. The understated presentation of those crises make them all the more moving. In "Send No Money" we see a man ruefully recalling his choice of the contemplative over the active life: "I thought wanting unfair; / It and finding out clash," he tells us. Now, half a lifetime later, he knows that only those who chose more active pursuits have any idea of "the way things go." All he knows is that truth is a "trite, untransferable Truss-advertisement," and that in his search he has squandered his youth.

II   *Poems of Assertion*

Approximately half of Larkin's poems develop in terms of the behavior or experience of characters; they seem designed to arouse appropriate emotions toward the feelings, actions, or situations they reveal. Most of the remaining poems are structured more in terms of assertions about the world outside. They reflect the poet's desire to make us see certain things in a certain way. In them the speaking voice is generally reliable. The reader of "Essential Beauty," "The Large Cool Store," or "Sunny Prestatyn" should come away from those poems with somewhat altered feelings about the billboards, cheap nightgowns, or railway posters most of us either scorn or ignore. Larkin encourages us to take them seriously as appeals to our painfully unrealistic notions of how life and love ought to be. Rather than prompting action or even necessarily conscious assent, such poems reinforce ways of seeing which relate to feelings we as readers share with the poet. Accordingly, the method of such poems is primarily rhetorical.

Many of these rhetorical poems exhibit the same degree of realistic detail to be found in "Church Going" or "The Whitsun Weddings." A few depend almost entirely for their effectiveness upon the force with which such detail is rendered. "Friday Night in the Royal Station Hotel" describes the deserted lobby, conference rooms, and corridors: empty chairs facing each other, full ashtrays, and the "larger loneliness of knives and glass / And silence laid like carpet." The panoramic view of northern England in "Here" rests on impressions of the countryside accumulated through the mind's eye, "Swerving east, from rich industrial shadows / And traffic all night north," until it reaches the "surprise of a large town." Such rural impressions are rural only in a marginal sense, for one must drive long to leave the "rich industrial shadows" of the nearest city, and even then reminders of modern encroachment on the once-deserted countryside abound. Scarcely is the city left when the provincial town surprises, and that town—with its "cut-price crowd, urban yet simple . . . [who] . . . / Push through plate-glass swing doors to their desires"—seems hardly very inspiring. Then the poem takes us far out of town to "isolate villages" not far from a beach, where Larkin ironically concludes: "Here is unfenced existence: / Facing the sun, untalkative, out of reach." Population and industry have taken over virtually all of the land. Only the sea remains "unfenced."

Implicit is the poet's frustrated search for the rural England preceding modern times, a search not unlike that of D. H. Lawrence. The realistic description of "Here" is matched in depth, if not breadth, in "Ambulances." In his recorded comments Larkin has called ambulances "ubiquitous moving rooms."[6] In the poem he initially sees them "Closed like confessionals," objects of universal curiosity and awe, which mysteriously "thread" their way through the city, ignoring "the glances they absorb," and "[coming] to rest at any kerb." He notes the intentness of the spectators as the "wild white face" is "stowed," their momentary sense of "the solving emptiness / That lies just under all we do." Their whispered sympathy he attributes to self-pity, claiming that we intimate our demise in the patient's death. According to Larkin, the ambulance "[b]rings closer what is left to come, / And dulls to distance all we are." The gradual shift from the ambulance's exterior to the crowd, and finally to a "we" which includes poet and reader, helps us share this insight. Contrary to the uniting experience of the speaker in "The Whitsun Weddings," our watching an ambulance is a dissolving experience. Because the death of another respresents a loosening of "the unique random blend / Of families and fashions" which defined him, we sense our own lives beginning to unravel.

A pair of poems built on similar rhetorical principles are "The Building" and "The Old Fools." Where the title in "Ambulances" identifies its subject and makes its metaphors immediately meaningful, in "The Building" Larkin begins with two stanzas of description which force the reader to discover, to his horror, what the poem is about:

> Higher than the handsomest hotel
> The lucent comb shows up for miles, but see,
> All round it close-ribbed streets rise and fall
> Like a great sigh out of the last century.
> The porters are scruffy; what keep drawing up
> At the entrances are not taxis; and in the hall
> As well as creepers hangs a frightening smell.
>
> There are paperbacks, and tea at so much a cup,
> Like an airport lounge, but those who tamely sit
> On rows of steel chairs turning the ripped mags
> Haven't come far. More like a local bus,
> These outdoor clothes and half-filled shopping bags
> And faces restless and resigned. . . .

At whatever point the reader realizes this is a hospital, he senses the critical difference between such a place and the other stations of life with which it is compared. Later Larkin notes the maze of stairways, corridors, and rooms making up the hospital, and speaks of the ill as the "unseen congregation whose white rows / Lie set apart above—women, men; / Old, young; crude facts of the only

coin / This place accepts." Finally he suggests that the hospital is
not unlike a cathedral, where crowds turn up each evening with
"wasteful, weak propitiatory flowers," trying to placate the forces of
life and death. Not until this final stanza does he mention death, the
common concern of all who gather there, or the fact that the
hospital, like the ambulance of the other poem, serves as a grim
reminder of their ultimate common fate—"Not yet, perhaps not
here, but in the end / And somewhere like this."

The peculiar starkness of the hospital as Larkin describes it stems
in part from his careful control of the speaking voice. For the first
two-thirds of the poem he gives us, in a detached manner, a grimly
sophisticated picture of the building and its occupants:

> Here to confess that something has gone wrong.
> It must be error of a serious sort,
> For see how many floors it needs, how tall
> It's grown by now, and how much money goes
> In trying to correct it.

This uncynical detachment continues until the seventh stanza,
when after surveying the ordinary scene outside the hospital window he suddenly bursts out:

> O world,
> Your loves, your chances, are beyond the stretch
> Of any hand from here! And so, unreal,
> A touching dream to which we all are lulled
> But wake from separately.

As in "Ambulances" Larkin waits for an appropriate point well into
the poem before admitting that the most real event in life may be
its conclusion and that the people he describes include himself and
his reader. His emotional outburst and return to calm reinforce that
admission, almost as a subplot of the poem.

"The Old Fools" makes similar use of the shifting voice. The first
stanza begins by asking, "What do they think has happened, the old
fools, / To make them like this?" and goes on to chronicle a variety
of senile mannerisms—drooling, uncontrolled urinating, seemingly
drunken walk, dumb stares—and to ask again, "Why aren't they
screaming?" After moving through a Lucretian description of dying
and declaring that the mannerisms he has observed are "first signs"
of imminent death, he develops a theory to explain the senile

patients' seeming obliviousness to their condition and the death it
portends: he sees them living in distant chambers of memory, unaware that they lie at the base of "extinction's alp." But even this
fails to satisfy him as he wonders whether at some point during the
"whole hideous inverted childhood" they don't realize the horrible
truth of their situation. "Well," he abruptly concludes, "[W]e shall
find out."

This conclusion ties together the feeling Larkin has tried to impart throughout the poem. Having pointed our attention not simply
to the ridiculousness of senile behavior but to the curious unconcern
of the senile, and having posed a theory which only begs the question, he leaves us with the reminder that if we cannot know now, we
can ultimately. As in "The Building" distancing devices of tone and
diction yield finally to a genuine sympathy, giving the initial
questions a more than impersonal interest.

Several of Larkin's other poems also operate from a realistic scene
or event, through reflective comment, to a loose conclusion.
Proceeding from the authoritative headnote from Mayhew,
"Deceptions" works through a sympathetic recounting of a
recruited child prostitute's feelings and by indirection to the question of who was more deceived, she or her attacker. Though
Larkin's real subject is self-deception engendered by desire, he continues to attend to the suffering girl. Understatement and continuing recognition of the outrage she suffered, rather than merely
overt statement or argument, persuade us to agree.

One of the most moving poems with this kind of rhetorical structure is "Faith Healing," written after Larkin watched a documen-
tary on that subject.[7] Characteristically he fastens our attention not
on the phoniness of the healer or the stupidity of the faithful, but on
the psychological significance of what happens to them, a
significance universalized in the final stanza. After describing the
appearance and manner of the faith-healer and the immediate
response of the women to the words of comfort, he notes, in
thoughtful detail, their secondary reactions as they begin to return
to their seats. They cry

> With deep hoarse tears, as if a kind of dumb
> And idiot child within them still survives
> To re-awake at kindness, thinking a voice
> At last calls them alone, that hands have come

> To lift and lighten; and such joy arrives
> Their thick tongues blort, their eyes squeeze grief, a crowd
> Of huge unheard answers jam and rejoice—

Where in "The Old Fools" his curiosity about the strange behavior he observes went unsatisfied, because he was excluded from the experience it signaled, here he recognizes in the women's tears the universal wish to be more loved:

> That nothing cures. An immense slackening ache,
> As when, thawing, the rigid landscape weeps,
> Spreads slowly through them—that, and the voice above
> Saying *Dear child*, and all time has disproved.

He sees in the appeal of the faith-healer and the tearful joy of the suppliants a reflection of general human regret. The healing which occurs is only momentary, creating an illusion of beneficent order which reality almost immediately begins to dispel.

Of course, many of Larkin's poems of assertion are much more compressed. Though working from the realistic scene of young mothers in the park, "Afternoons" involves much less physical description and no shift of tone in suggesting that "Something is pushing them / To the side of their own lives." Similarly, poems like "Talking in Bed" and "Nothing To Be Said" rely more on emblematic detail than on the profusion of realistic description found in the longer poems; in each the sense of futility the poet would impart is matched by a spareness of concrete description. The same is true in "Wants," where the mention of invitation-cards and the family photograph "under the flagstaff" detracts not at all from the stark "desire of oblivion" the poem is intended to suggest. Even "Home is so Sad," which depends on cited domestic objects, does so only at the end of a series of terse, unembroidered statements. And "As Bad as a Mile" consists of a single, uncomplicated declaration:

> Watching the shied core
> Striking the basket, skidding across the floor,
> Shows less and less of luck, and more and more
>
> Of failure spreading back up the arm
> Earlier and earlier, the unraised hand calm,
> The apple unbitten in the palm.

While conveying little sense of urgency, such poems move rather quickly to their conclusions, to achieve an almost epigrammatic effect.

Some of Larkin's best rhetorical poems obtain their effects by the distance which metaphor places between them and concrete reality. An early example is the "Two Portraits of Sex" included in *XX Poems*, the second part of which became "Dry Point" in *The Less Deceived*. While it is difficult to know why Larkin included only the second portrait in the later collection, by itself it may better represent his attitude. Certainly the style of "Dry Point" is more characteristic of the mature Larkin manner. At any rate, in their original positions the two portraits, titled "Oils" and "Etching," suggest converse ways of regarding sex. The first portrait consists of a forceful but impersonal tribute to the power and importance of the sexual principle:

> Barn-clutch of life. Trigger of the future.
> Magic weed the doctor shakes in the dance.
>
> . . . .
>
> New voice saying new words at a new speed
> From which the future erupts like struck oil,
>
> . . . .
>
> No one can tie you down or set you free.
> Apart from your tribe, there is only the dead,
> And even them you grip and begin to use.

The poem offers no concrete description, but rather a series of suggestive phrases. And, what it suggests is not so much sex as a way of regarding it. Then, in "Etching," Larkin undercuts that romantic viewpoint by a stark address to the "time-honored irritant" sex as a repeatedly disappointed intruder.

Metaphorical correlatives are a necessity in representing such feelings. To attempt to render them through realism would be absurd. This is why "Next, Please" seems such an appropriate representation of the painful anticipation consuming most of life. Larkin succinctly captures this feeling by picturing it as a figurative bluff upon which we eagerly await that big ship—"leaning with brasswork primped, / Each rope distinct, / Flagged, and the figurehead with golden tits"—which never lands. Even more surreal but equally compelling is his image in "Whatever Happened?"

of standing on deck—"With trousers ripped, light wallet, and lips bleeding"—after moving through a disastrous "latitude." But, probably his most surrealistic poem is "The Card Players," a recent work parodying Dutch genre-painting, to suggest the distinction between appearance and reality even in the world of a painting.

III   *Poems of Argument*

The third class of structures employed by Larkin is argument. Because argumentative poems develop with more logical tightness than poems of action or assertion, they seem designed more to spur the reader to action or at least to rational assent. Two of his most recent poems, "Homage to a Government" and "Going, Going," illustrate this logical structuring, as well as his later shift toward greater topicality in his writing.

The first of these was originally published in the *Sunday Times*, apparently to express disapproval over the Labour government's 1968 reduction in military expenditures.[8] In the opening stanza Larkin announces, "Next year we are to bring the soldiers home / For lack of money, and it is all right." This pose of the acquiescent observer continues as he outlines the publicly stated reasons for closing various military bases abroad: the money is needed at home, the places are remote from Britain, British troops are not popular there. "Next year we shall be easier in our minds," he agrees, to close the second stanza.

Then, using "next year" as a wedge, he drives home the attack he has kept hidden:

> Next year we shall be living in a country
> That brought its soldiers home for lack of money.
> The statues will be standing in the same
> Tree-muffled squares, and look nearly the same.
> Our children will not know it's a different country.
> All we can hope to leave them now is money.

Whether the withdrawals *per se* disturb Larkin is difficult to tell, although in a couplet published about the same time he offered pragmatic objection to military cuts: "When the Russian tanks roll westward, what defence for you and me? / Colonel Sloman's Essex Rifles? The Light Horse of L.S.E.?"[9] Certainly the circumstances and justification for withdrawal make him suspicious. "Homage to a

Government" operates much more syllogistically than the assertive poems examined earlier. Implicit are the premises that the nation which sacrifices moral responsibility for material expediency is doomed to moral decay and that the British pullouts are founded on such principles of expediency.

The more recent protest poem, "Going, Going," refers to another alarming development in Britain, the threat to the natural environment. Again rhetoric reinforces logical structure, as Larkin assumes the position of the modest observer who thought the old countryside would survive his lifetime and who even wonders if perhaps his age is making him an alarmist. Having registered this stance, rather early in the poem, he goes on to note the suburban and business spillovers into previously "unspoilt" areas, and to confess

> It seems, just now,
> To be happening, so very fast;
> Despite all the land left free
> For the first time I feel somehow
> That it isn't going to last,
>
> That before I snuff it, the whole
> Boiling will be bricked in
> Except for the tourist parts—

As in "Homage to a Government," Larkin here points to signs of Britain's imminent decay. In both poems he writes for readers who may not be aware of the full significance of such developments. In each instance he cites selfishness and greed as the motives behind the alarming developments. Presumably his intended audience is neither selfish nor greedy, and, if alerted, will act in some appropriate way. In concluding that "greeds / And garbage are too thick-strewn / To be swept up now, or invent / Excuses that make them all needs," he calls for a last effort to arrest these alarming symptoms of England's demise.

Some of his less topical poems are also structured logically. The conclusion reached in "An Arundel Tomb," that "What will survive of us is love," follows directly from the speaker's observations and reflections. A shorter poem, "Ignorance," is almost straight syllogism, as it begins by establishing uncertainty as strange, proceeds to define our relationship to our bodies as one of uncertainty—"our flesh / Surrounds us with its own decisions— / And yet [we] spend all our life on imprecisions, / That when we start to

die / Have no idea why"—and so implies that such a relationship is
indeed strange. The detailed photographic scene of English life at
the very edge of World War I in "MCMXIV" leads to the refrain,
"Never such innocence, / Never before or since. . . ." Similarly
"Show Saturday" moves through the profusion of peculiarities and
customs of the country show to remind the reader that it is
"something they share / That breaks ancestrally each year into / Regenerate union," and to urge "Let it always be there." And
in "To the Sea" he calls attention to the summer migration of
Britishers as a valued link between eras and generations. "Still going on, all of it still going on!" he exclaims, as he recalls his own
seaside adventures as a child. "Let it always be there," he seems to
conclude again.

With "Livings" Larkin offers three vignettes juxtaposing the artificial existences of the small businessman and Oxford don against
the hearty life of the British seafarer. The first speaker describes his
typical evening in a provincial town, noting familiar objects and
guests at the hotel, and reveals his sense of purposelessness in his
work:

> I drowse
> Between ex-Army sheets, wondering why
> I think it's worth while coming. Father's dead;
> He used to, but the business now is mine.
> It's time for change. . . .

Significantly this poem is set in 1929. David Timms sees in the style
and diction of the third "Living" a suggestion of 1829.[10] In it a
young don characterizes his evening of academic smalltalk in the
college dining room as no more stimulating than that endured by
the businessman.

In between we have the seaman's soliloquy, distinguished from
the others by a liveliness of tone and rhythm:

> Seventy feet down
> The sea explodes upwards,
> Relapsing, to slaver
> Off landing-stage steps—
> Running suds, rejoice!
>
> Rocks writhe back to sight.
> Mussels, limpets,

> Husband their tenacity
> In the freezing slither—
> Creatures, I cherish you!

Through the contrast of style and attitude, Larkin revives the occupational issue dealt with in the Toads poems. He suggests the importance of a vital vocation in any work. While the seaman is truly caught up in his situation, the others merely fill time in theirs.

This conclusion is implicit. A small group of other poems work entirely through analogy to imply logical conclusions. Each suggests a parallel or significant difference between human life and some nonhuman phenomenon. "Wires" quietly but effectively compares how such fences age the young animals with how life jars us from our youthful ambitions and fantasies. Like "Wires," "First Sight" develops a comparison between the growing pains of men and animals, in this instance lambs. But here, though, the suggestion is that just as lambs learning to walk in snow are misled into underrating the possibilities of life, so are children in judging by their necessarily limited experience. Both will learn the wonder of "[e]arth's immeasurable surprise":

> They could not grasp it if they knew,
> What so soon will wake and grow
> Utterly unlike the snow.

Larkin here seems to undercut the myth of childhood from the other end, to suggest that adulthood holds perhaps a lesser proportion of pain, and certainly more variety.

"At Grass" is a more lengthily drawn comparison—actually a contrast—between the manner of retired racehorses and men:

> Do memories plague their ears like flies?
> They shake their heads. . . .
> Almanacked, their names live; they
>
> Have slipped their names, and stand at ease,
> Or gallop for what must be joy,
> And not a fieldlglass sees them home,
> Or curious stop-watch prophesies. . . .

Some question has been raised as to whether thesse horses are to represent a potential state of mind for man, as well as an unflattering contrast. It is suggested that Larkin perhaps means to have it both ways, to imply that man can and cannot enjoy this kind of peace.[11]

While such a reading is plausible, the ease with which the horses accept the passing of their glory depends upon their subhumanity. Presumably their jockeys, trainers, and others directly dependent upon their winnings have been much less oblivious to their retirement. Certainly regret for the passing of time and glory is probable in the world of Larkin's poetry; for numerous reasons his characters can never approach the contentment of a Rabbi Ben Ezra. At best they achieve a standoff against regret. Perhaps the key to this particular poem is the speaker himself. In a real sense he projects his ideals onto the horses, attributing human motives to their shaking of heads much as does Frost's speaker in "Stopping by Woods on a Snowy Evening." His noticing the horses in this way suggests regret that man cannot be like them. The poem reminds us how hopelessly unlike the horses we are.

Some of Larkin's didactic poems operate by parody. Through exaggerated imitation he satirizes the folly of a type or attitude. His fierce dislike of academic gamesmanship is seen in "Naturally the Foundation Will Bear Your Expenses" and "Posterity." The traveling lecturer of the first poem recalls passing through London to catch a plane and being delayed by Armistice Day ceremonies—"Wreath-rubbish in Whitehall" and "mawkish nursery/ games," he calls them. He asks, "O when will England grow up?" His insensitivity to the feeling behind such patriotic traditions and his preoccupation with his own academic games becomes even more pronounced in his way of resolving his annoyance:

> But I outsoar the Thames,
> And dwindle off down Auster
> To greet Professor Lal
> (He once met Morgan Forster),
> My contact and my pal.

The invoking of Forster's name by one so indifferent to humane values is especially ironic.

Such indifference becomes scorn with his American counterpart, Larkin's imagined biographer, who grumbles about being "stuck with this old fart at least a year" in deference to the tenure game.

He expresses impatience with the ordinariness of his subject and vows: "Just let me put this bastard on the skids, / I'll get a couple of semesters leave / to work on Protest Theater." Both poems object sharply to the shallowness and intellectual hypocrisy of literary academicism.

In "A Study of Reading Habits" Larkin more charitably satirizes the simpleminded approach to reading taken by most people. The character's disappointment with books reveals not only his disillusionment with life in general, but the fallacy of reading to find a mirror of oneself. And yet, as Larkin suggests elsewhere, literature should address real human problems and feelings. How else, therefore, can the reader approach a story or poem but by his own feelings? The poem suggests the dilemma of combining involvement with perspective, a dilemma the speaker is totally unable to handle. Certainly, though, he projects greater sincerity than the more sophisticated academicians of the other two satirical poems.

CHAPTER 5

Style and Technique

I T is both necessary and difficult to talk about style and technique in Philip Larkin's poetry. Necessary, because they are the center of much of the critical controversy surrounding his work, as well as a major factor in his popularity. Difficult, because, in keeping with the attitudes he brings to his writing, his style is, for the most part, not readily obvious. It is a style designed to hide itself behind the human situation and emotions revealed in the poems, a style founded on the assumption that the average reader of reasonable intelligence should be able to understand and enjoy poetry and that the poet's technique should never assert itself to complicate unnecessarily such understanding or enjoyment.

Because of Larkin's wariness toward academic attitudes in poetry, in the arts, and in life in general, to discuss the method of his poems becomes almost a betrayal of the spirit in which they were composed; more than most poets, a dissection of Larkin seems to require murder. At the same time, also more than with most poets, such dissection obligates the critic to regard subject and context even as he discusses technical matters; Larkin's poems refuse to be murdered easily. The impossibility, or at least the folly, of separating style and content, which Larkin has suggested in his critical remarks, is thus forcefully demonstrated through his own poetry.

I *Voice*

This inseparability accounts for the feeling of many of Larkin's readers and critics that, whatever the limitations of his viewpoint, he is sincere. The speaking voice of his poems comes across as natural, encouraging the reader to believe that the style is indeed the man and that it represents a man with whom one can identify and from whom one can learn. This is not to suggest that Larkin's

91

poetry is formally didactic—our examination of structure suggests
that usually it is not—but that the reliable personae in many of his
poems, as well as the implied authority behind his unreliable
speakers, is not only a man speaking to men, but a sensitive and
sympathetic sharer of life's pain and joy. Dan Jacobson has commented on the "novelistic" nature of much of Larkin's poetry,[1]
referring to its emphasis on concrete situation and realistic detail. In
a larger sense most of Larkin's poems remind us of the novel—and
particularly the traditional English novel epitomized by George
Eliot, Hardy, or Lawrence—in that their narrators and commen-
tators exhibit both perspective and empathy with what they
describe.

Such naturalness obviously depends upon the words which the
poet uses, words marking Larkin as a citizen of the world familiar to
most of his readers. If, as suggested earlier, the world of his poetry is
a contemporary British world, the voice by which that world is
presented seems very much that of an insider. Thus Larkin's people
can speak very informally. The feeling that the young man in "If,
My Darling" is basically reliable and well-meaning derives in part
from the details of his confession, whereby a "grecian statue kicked
in the privates" represents for him his own disloyalty, and he
defends his decision not to confess to his "darling" by claiming that
it might knock her off "her unpriceable pivot." A sympathetic bond
between the reader and even less reliable characters is created by
their saying things like "Stuff your pension!" ("Toads"), "Get
stewed!" ("A Study of Reading Habits"), or "Sod all" ("Send No
Money") to vent their frustrations. The hapless bachelor in "Self's
the Man," for all of his shortsightedness, convinces us of the basic
humanity from which his dilemma springs when he says that poor
Arnold's domestic burden, in comparison with his own freedom,
makes him "feel a swine," or that he is a "better hand" at knowing
the limits of his tolerance "Without them sending a van." Such
commonplace expressions in context mark their users as unpreten-
tious even when misguided.

Perhaps the most extreme instance of advantageously used slang
comes in "Sunny Prestatyn," which recounts the demise of the
swim-suited girl in a travel poster through the efforts of a graffitist
signing himself "Titch Thomas":

> A couple of weeks, and her face
> Was snaggle-toothed and boss-eyed;
> Huge tits and a fissured crotch

> Were scored well in, and the space
> Between her legs held scrawls
> That set her fairly astride
> A tuberous cock and balls

The blunt language of these lines suggests a basic agreement between Larkin and the unknown Titch Thomas; for both poet and graffitist such terms better represent the real world of frustration and disappointment than does the false promise of the poster. As usual, Larkin sympathizes with those to whom the poster would appeal, as well as with the disillusionment registered through the obscene drawings. His terms describing the altered poster, coupled with the sad observation that the girl was "too good for this life" and that now "*Fight Cancer* is there," help convince us that Titch was at least less deceived and less deceiving, and that his actions represent more than gratuitous vandalism. Indeed, Larkin implies that all spontaneous human gestures, and especially those regarding such basic matters as sex and death, deserve respectful attention. The attitudes represented by the obscene drawings constitute at least as valid an approach to life—and for Larkin certainly a more honest one—than the romanticism of the original poster. The recourse to slang in many of his poems suggests his recognition that the language of the street is more honest than that of the academy.

This respect for the common man's language does not mean a surrender to such language or to total informality. Rather, it means a healthy skepticism toward an overly artificial or overly academic view of life or poetry, and a determination to say things in no more esoteric terms than necessary. The diction and style of Larkin's poems can mostly be characterized as middle-level, in keeping with their generally neutral tone. "Sunny Prestatyn" itself illustrates his tendency to mix the formal with the informal, since the graphic sexual terms of the poem are surrounded by much less slangy diction. The stream of slang from Jake Balakowsky in "Posterity," as a departure from Larkin's usual practice, thus reinforces the poem's satirical intention.

The quiet, almost conversational quality of most of his poems depends on the orderly but relaxed arrangement of fairly ordinary diction. But, as Lolette Kuby has pointed out, "simplicity does not mean simplexity."[2] The simple appearance of almost all his poems is deceptive; it means only that they can be read, not that they can be fully comprehended, in a brief time. Larkin's is a poetry which, while proving meaningful on first reading, rewards with subsequent readings. This power to produce additional significance with additional reading depends largely upon his careful selection of words which in context give off a variety of nuances and connotations. In his choice of such language, he is decidedly in step with modern poetic theory, particularly that of the New Critics. In fact, what Larkin has amusingly pointed out about John Betjeman's verse, that it is a "kind of distorting mirror in which all the catch-phrases of modern criticism appear in gross unacceptable parody,"[3] might just as well be said about his own poems. His thorough integration into his verse of what from a less skilled poet might seem blatantly "symbolic" or "poetic" elements relates him especially, and ironically, to Yeats: his achieving a more natural, less obtrusive diction in his mature poems suggests that he cast off Yeats on thoroughly Yeatsian grounds.

Just as the surface simplicity of Larkin's writing does not keep him from dealing with complex questions, it does not prevent him at strategic points from using a more elaborate diction or a more elevated style. Sometimes such a style is in keeping with the dignified subjects and impersonal points of view taken in the poems. In "An Arundel Tomb," it seems quite appropriate to speak of death as a "supine stationary voyage," just as periphrasis—"Wretched width of cold" or "Earth's immeasurable surprise"—seems similarly proper to the intent of "First Sight." And, the talk of "propitiatory flowers" and other Latinate diction befit the elaborate development of "The Building." Even when the immediate subject is not particularly or traditionally dignified, Larkin can make it so through an elevated vocabulary. One is reminded almost of classical pastorals when he invests the retired racehorses in "At Grass" with the status of superhuman ideals for restless man. Part of this investure comes in his noting how the wind "distresses tail and mane," or how one of the horses "crops" grass. Such details, as well as the slow progression of description and reflection, reinforce the sense of significance he would give the horses.

Sometimes a single abstract or technical word, rather than appearing out of place, will help elevate a potentially trivial situation to the level of universal significance. Such seems to be the case with the use of "cicatrized" early in Larkin's account of stopping a diary ("Forget What Did") or "supperate," to give a clinical dimension to human helplessness ("Myxomatosis"). Extensive reliance on abstractions reinforces the serious philosophical meaning in poems like "Triple Time" and "Age," where Larkin bridges the gap between problems perplexing us all in our daily lives and the metaphysical issues to which they are related.

Of course, while he can use highly informal language, as well as highly formal, his usual practice is to mix them strategically in a single poem. This is what Edna Langley means when she commends his "Yeatsian" mastery of big words and his ability to integrate them with a conversational idiom reminiscent of Edward Thomas.[4] In "Places, Loved Ones," the speaker tells, in serious, formal tones, of never having found a special person or place, and of how such a discovery might relieve him of choice and responsibility. Yet, he uses words like "dolt" and "mashed" to reveal his underlying disdain for his circumstances. In "Essential Beauty" he uses contrasting modes of diction to distinguish the ideal image of billboards, "those sharply-pictured groves," from the imperfect real world they mock, suggested by the boy "puking his heart out in the Gents." The jazz-lover in "For Sidney Bechet" seems to contrast the feeble response of academics—"[S]cholars *manques* . . . unnoticed/ Wrapped up in personnels like old plaids . . ."—with the earthier images of "sporting-house girls like paper tigers" others find in the music. A similar mix vitally reinforces the contrast between the desired rebellion and rationalized conformity in "Poetry of Departures." The informal language of the poem—"He chucked up everything / And just cleared off" or "Take that, you bastard"—is relegated to italicized "fifth-hand" quotation by the speaker, who is forced by character and circumstance to limit his own remarks to a polite language indicative of the order he detests but cannot escape. In "Sad Steps" the informal first line, "Groping back to bed after a piss," establishes a candor which combines in succeeding lines with a high seriousness and a profoundly disturbing realization expressed in appropriately formal tones. This same effect is created by the references early in "High Windows" to "fucking," "taking pills," and going down the slide "Like free bloody birds," which gradually give way to metaphysical concerns. The base of sincerity created by informal language permits Larkin to pursue serious subjects without seeming stuffy. While eschewing vulgarity, he avoids the greater dangers of turgidity and excessive academicism inherent in the kinds of poems he writes.

One stylistic quality noted by many critics and indicative of the Larkin cast of mind is his tendency toward negative qualifiers, and especially his reliance on the prefix "un." In "Born Yesterday" he wishes the infant an "unemphasized" happiness, while elsewhere he speaks of someone being "untruthful" and "unfingermarked," and of things being "uncustomary," "unrecompensed," and "unclosing." Relatedly, in "The Importance of Elsewhere" he distinguishes between feeling "separate" and feeling "unworkable," citing the latter as his usual situation. Such avoidance of positives reflects a preference for whittling things down to their true dimensions and qualities, even at the risk of understatement. Because, as he implies in all of his poems, man tends to delusion about himself and life and thereby invites personal disaster, perhaps the most valuable service poetry can render as representer of truth is to remind us of this danger even in the very words used to describe the world of the poem. The poet thus teaches by example as much as by precept.

This use of the negative prefix is compounded in Larkin's use of double-negatives, again to avoid rendering things in any more positive terms than their reality can bear. Having described the words lovers seek with increasing difficulty as "at once true and kind," he rephrases his description to read, "not untrue and not unkind," thus reducing such words to the level of impossibility ("Talking in Bed"). So, too, speaking to the newborn in "Born Yesterday," rather than using terms like "normal" or "well-rounded"—which would emphasize the positive virtues of what he wishes—he asks for her "nothing uncustomary," preferring even the negative, "dullness," to the positives he distrusts.

Of course, any discussion of diction without an accompanying consideration of syntax ignores a vital part of Larkin's easy but deliberate manner. The fact that his verse is written mostly in simple, complete sentences is symptomatic of that ease and deliberateness. Equally significant is what Lolette Kuby describes as the disposition of Larkin's speakers to dialectical and eristic exposition. Questions and answers or outright debate characterize the mode of many poems already examined. As Ms. Kuby suggests, these forms of exposition represent ways not only of testing the truth of a given position and its counter, but of suggesting the partial truth of both: "[T]he poet says two things at once, neither of which is entirely true or entirely untrue and which, in effect, test the truth of each other. The persona can change his mind, but in the poem, as Larkin writes it, what is said cannot be unsaid."[5] His occasional use of a word like "well" or "so"—for example, "So your old name shelters our faithfulness" ("Maiden Name")—signals not only the approaching end of the poem, but the end of a process of comparing and weighing such partial truths. Sometimes such a word reinforces our sense of their partiality, as when the character in "Wild Oats" concludes, "Well, useful to get that learned," to suggest caustically that he has learned nothing for certain except what he knew at the beginning, that he is alone and unhappy. This dialectic of qualification and reduction making up so many Larkin poems Edna Langley has termed "agnosticism in practice,"[6] for it clearly reflects his distrust of hyperbole and absolutes, as well as his insistence on an honest facing of unpleasant truths.

Syntactical shifts within poems are another means by which Larkin reinforces structure and meaning. In "Forget What Did" he moves from declarative sentences, through a question, to end with a conditional statement. Having concentrated initially on the wisdom of stopping his diary, he then speculates on the significance of the remaining "empty pages," before concluding that "should they ever be filled" it will be with things he can bear remembering. This shift of grammatical mood reinforces the sense of the emptiness of his personal life and the tenuousness of his defense against despair. Likewise the young bride in "Wedding Wind" moves from fairly long sentences with coordinate clauses to much shorter statements, to suggest the difference between the expansive optimism of her wedding night and the uncertainty of the morning after, before asking the series of questions with which the poem concludes. A similar syntactical principle seems at work in another early poem, "Latest Face," where the final section contains a series of increasingly drawn-out questions, to represent the speaker's increasing perplexity. These few examples illustrate the functional variety of sentence patterns implicit in almost all the poems.

II *Imagery*

Like his diction and syntax, imagery and figurative language in Larkin's poetry can go unnoticed as such, so much do they operate as natural parts of character and situation. Because of his disdain for the poetic extremes resulting from the modernist rubrics of Imagism and Symbolism, many of Larkin's more figurative poems seem strangely literal—literal because he generally avoids levels of meaning much divorced from the surface situation or problem, and strangely so because almost all of his poetry, even as it appears consistently literal, with equal consistency suggests a universality of reference. Lolette Kuby points out that Larkin uses realism in much the same way that Pound, Yeats, and Eliot used Imagism, Gaelic mythology, and Christian beliefs respectively, as the basis for larger meaning.[7] Larkin's poems almost always have the effect of meaning more than they say, and of referring somehow to more than they mention.

The explanation for this subtle nonliteralism—or delusive literalism—lies partly in the subjects with which his poems and characters deal; they literally are a part of the lives of most readers. But even so, to them Larkin adds a measure of symbolic suggestiveness rising out of the very details in the poems themselves. Frequently objects and words take on an extraliteral meaning for the reader because they obviously do for the speaker. Thus the items catalogued in "MCMXIV" seem to symbolize aspects of the Edwardian life-style because the speaker treats them lovingly and reverently as symbols. Similarly, the many details cited in "Going, Going"—or, for that matter, in "To the Sea" and "Show Saturday"—suffice to suggest an entire way of life in England.

It is ironic to notice, therefore, that by many definitions of figurative or symbolic language such poems, for all of their quiet but intense emotion, are decidedly denotative and transparent. The images which the middle-aged man in "High Windows" carries in his mind as he finally turns his attention—the windows themselves, of "sun-comprehending glass," and the "deep blue air"—immediately represent for us the metaphysical dimension of human questing, the ultimate which religion seeks to embrace, because the character obviously sees them as such. Likewise, because the details of Arnold's life mentioned in "Self's the Man" represent for Larkin's dissatisfied speaker the whole domestic routine, we accept them as sufficiently representative. Having repeatedly insisted that a poet must, above all, be a man, Larkin seems to imply through such poems as these that a man, by virtue of his humanness, will be a poet, at least to himself. In a sense such poems involve the reader's eavesdropping on the unwitting poetic composition of characters. We see the speaker select what for him are satisfactorily representative details. The poem causes us to reconstruct that which they represent.

Equally impressive is Larkin's penchant for integrating conventionally figurative language into his poems. In "A Study of Reading Habits," the numerous slang metaphors—"my nose in a book," "the old right hook", "ripping times," "clubbed with sex," "the chap who's yellow and keeps the store"—all appear the perfectly natural result, or indication, of the speaker's station and attitude, so natural that they are scarcely recognizable as metaphors.

Larkin's puns, usually of great significance in their contexts, are likewise camouflaged, so that they work on the reader without his being aware of anything so mechanical as word-play.) In this category fall the sexually connotative phrase, "feel of girls," in "Reasons for Attendance," by which the speaker unwittingly foreshadows the frustration ultimately revealed, and the combination of the adverbial and the adjectival in the comment, "more and more time passes silently" ("Talking in Bed"), whereby the two meanings reinforce each other and the feeling of hopelessness Larkin aims to impart. Then there is the "great transverse tear" near the end of "Sunny Prestatyn," which initially seems another feature of the emended poster-girl's face, a mark of her supposed sorrow for what cannot be, but by the end of the poem seems intended to rhyme with "there" as a mark of Titch Thomas's scorn for the false promise she held out. In actuality it is both [tier] and [teer,] both subject and object, both appearance and reality. Perhaps the most refined instance of Larkin's punning comes in the "sad" of "Home is So Sad," as it reflects both the personality of the home and the regret of the speaker for his home.

Even when Larkin's skill with multiple meanings is more exposed, it operates naturally in the context of the particular poem. His comparison of himself to a child as he sees spring approaching ("Coming"), like his addressing the newborn child as "Tightly-folded bud" ("Born Yesterday"), blends with its context because it literally relates to the natural forces of rebirth and renewal occasioning the poem. Relatedly, the description of love as a glaring "much-remembered brilliance"—"Its bright incipience sailing above"—captures precisely the mood of the old love songs recalled by the widow, as does Larkin's account of her playing them:

> Relearning how each frank submissive chord
>   Had ushered in
> Word after sprawling hyphenated word,
> And the unfailing sense of being young
> Spread out like a spring-woken tree. . . .
>   ("Love Songs in Age")

Here again we see Larkin taking seriously a commonplace consumer product, in this case the popular song, as an appeal to everyman's dream. The terms with which he renders the widow's momentary renewal of youthful illusion capture the automatic, irresistible quality of that appeal, a "glare" complicating her ordinarily sober vision. In "Dockery and Son" the speaker's characterization of the things we think truest as "tight-shut, like doors" recalls the implicit symbolism earlier in the poem, where he finds "the door of where I used to live" locked. The locked door figures as a metaphor for the mysterious operations of time, fate, and character, leaving him hopelessly estranged from satisfaction with himself or his life.

Larkin's restraint in his use of figurative language makes it a telling if subtle tool. On occasion he does not hesitate to build a fairly elaborate metaphorical pattern. In such cases, though, the pattern becomes a self-characterizing device. Thus in "No Road" the speaker's embroidering the obvious metaphor of the unused road as the remnant of the once-thriving friendship, the homely references to bricking up gates and planting trees to enforce their parting, and the progress report of drifting leaves and creeping grass all mark the speaker himself as not only thoughtful, but as skillful in redeeming a potentially trite comparison into a very apt description of the relationship and the dilemma it poses. This kind of serious wit prepares the reader for the telling self-appraisal at the end of the poem. Perhaps exceptional among Larkin's poems in terms of its reliance on metaphor, "No Road" represents further evidence of his refusal to employ metaphor for any narrowly "poetic" effect, his determination to fuse poetic device and extrapoetic significance.

Many other poems exhibit internal patterning of figurative language, though usually on a more modest scale. Metaphorical cross-reference figures strongly in "Wedding-Wind," where the young bride employs two sets of metaphors—one natural or rural, the other religious—to express her combined joy and fear. She compares her blissful love to "kneeling as cattle by all-generous waters" and "a thread / Carrying beads," while wondering if the wind of death will dry up the waters or snap the thread.

The young man in "If, My Darling" builds his amusing expression of apprehension by a fairly elaborate comparison of his mind to a Victorian home distinguished, like the childhood in "I Remember, I Remember," for what it lacks. Shifting from what his darling would not find there to what she would, he quickly establishes his mind as a chamber of horrors, "looped with the creep of varying light," with an "unwholesome floor, as it might be the skin of the grave," and the "Grecian statue kicked in the privates." Witty description becomes increasingly surrealistic, with mixed metaphors, metaphors upon other metaphors, and a shift from sight to sound, to support his contention that his girl friend had best be locked out of his irrational consciousness. As in "No Road," the character's skill with metaphor alerts us to his wit, in the literary sense, which here saves him from despair and the poem from the straight pathos such a dilemma might evoke.

The extended address in "Skin" similarly casts the subject of aging—often the stimulas for hopelessness among Larkin's people—in an amusing, even comic light. Extended metaphor serves as an equally cohesive element in "Next, Please," with its repeated reference to waiting on shore for that ship of good fortune which never quite arrives, and in "Whatever Happened?", with its figure of personal disaster as the temporary fall overboard during the voyage of life. Larkin cements his argument in "Faith Healing" by shifting from the "warm spring rain of loving care" in the first stanza, suggestive of the healer, to the healed, whose crying he attributes to "An immense slackening ache, / As when, thawing, the rigid landscape weeps." This ironic shift suggests the ultimate futility of the faith-healer's efforts. Rather than the spring soil, eager for more moisture, the women in the scene become a frozen ground, whom further rain awakens not to love for others, but to self-pity in their insatiable want of love. While necessary, their catharsis brings no escape from the pathetic egoism which, according to Larkin, we all share to some degree.

Another interesting aspect of metaphor in Larkin's poetry is his way of strategically placing figurative language. In "Deceptions" the piling up of figures and images in the first part of the poem gives way to the almost nonimagistic starkness of the second, to parallel and reinforce the shift of subject, from sympathetic concern for the rape victim to a consideration of the rapist himself. The starkness of language in the second part of the poem underscores the emotional death which is the rapist's reward for his futile lusting.

Other poems employ an opposite shift with equal effectiveness. The character in "Church Going" employs no really figurative language until the final stanza, when he settles down to a more profound examination of his motives. This switch to metaphor suggests that heretofore in wondering why he stopped at such a place, he scarcely got beyond the superficial and flippant level of literalism in the poem's early stanzas. Likewise, the traveler in "The Whitsun Weddings" indicates his increased interest and emotional attachment to the newlyweds by an increased use of figurative language, contrasting with the colorful but literal realism of the opening stanzas. The final lines, in which the imminent setting-forth of the train's passengers is likened to "an arrow-shower / Sent out of sight, somewhere becoming rain," derive their profundity in part from the absence of such comparisons earlier in the poem. And, as is usual with Larkin, because the comparison is the speaker's and seems a natural result of his increasing emotion, the reader is made to feel that he has observed a plausible evolving of significance through scene and character, rather than the imposition of meaning by the poet.

III *Prosody*

The principle behind much of the prosodic element in Larkin's verse seems to be an unresolved tension between formal regularity and irregularity, and between subtlety and abrasiveness in the use of various devices. In this way technique parallels ideology, reminding us of various other basic tensions in the poems, such as that between the concern for security and the desire for excitement, or between the value placed on awareness and the need for sustaining illusions in life, or even between the urge to write and an underlying sense of the pointlessness of such activity. Larkin's greater commitment to traditional forms in comparison with other leading contemporary poets is misleading, since a close examination of his techniques reveals an insistent technical skepticism not unlike that with which he treats the more explicit issues of his poetry. He cannot fully affirm a "free-verse" position in his poems because he cannot honestly affirm freedom as a realizable or even fully desirable style of life. Nevertheless he implies a questioning attitude toward traditional technical controls even as he uses them.

His use of the stanza to subdivide his poems exemplifies this principle. Because almost all of his poems are written in stanzas of some sort, to the casual observer they appear very old-fashioned. Yet, the type of stanza is almost never the same from poem to poem, and within a given poem usually there is marked irregularity, even from the beginning, in rhyme or meter. Such is the frequent complexity of the Larkin stanza that it appears to be a satire itself on the whole idea of the stanza. By setting up the stanzaic form and deviating from it in so many ways without abandoning it entirely, Larkin seems to turn the form upside-down, to question its validity even while maintaining a formal appearance. Larkin is reported to have expressed the desire to write a poem of such stanzaic complexity as to permit wandering through the stanzas like the aisles and chapels of a cathedral.[8] Regardless of the accuracy of this report, some of his poems certainly invite a degree of such wandering, as their stanzas include deviations calculated to make the reader lose track of, or faith in, the overall pattern itself.

Syntax operates as the foremost underminer of the Larkin stanza. Almost never do sentences correspond exactly to stanzas; in most poems they spill over from stanza to stanza, giving the reader the sense not only of competing organizational principles, but of the sentence as a vehicle of meaning taking over the poem. "At Grass," "Church Going," "The Whitsun Weddings," and "High Windows" are but a few of the dozens of poems in which the stanza is extensively offset by enjambment between stanzas and caesura within them. In "I Remember, I Remember," where only the first and last stanzas end with a period, Larkin very strategically continues stanza-division and enjambment between the final line of the fourth stanza and the beginning of the fifth—

> And here we have that splendid family
>
> I never ran to when I got depressed,
> The boys all biceps and the girls all chest,

to support, by surprise, probably the wittiest part of his poem. Likewise, in "Dockery and Son" the disparity between stanza and sentence throughout the poem reinforces the uncertainty informing the character's meditation.

Of course, such spillover between stanzas usually occurs relatively late in the poem, to disturb not only a comfortable stanzaic pattern but the line of thought pursued up to that point. Not until midway through "An Arundel Tomb" is the pattern of end-stopped stanzas broken to help divert the reader's attention from the external details of the sculpture to its ironic significance. A late break in stanza-sentence correspondence reinforces a similar shift in "The Explosion," from a fairly realistic account of the disaster to a more surrealistic description of its appearance to survivors. And, though enjambment carries no definitive significance, it surely is no coin-

cidence that most of those poems containing only end-stopped stanzas—such as "Naturally the Foundation . . .," "Take One Home
for the Kiddies," and "A Study of Reading Habits"—follow basically satirical intentions.

Other techniques mitigate against the strict stanza, to help create
the same kind of tension encouraged by enjambment. In "Dockery
and Son" Larkin twice combines the spillover from one stanza with
caesura in the first line of the next, to underscore the central symbols of the poem, the locked door and the "unhindered" moon.
This same combination operates frequently in "Wedding-Wind" to
reinforce key words and phrases in the speaker's meditation placed
strategically at the beginning of particular lines. "Mr. Bleaney" exhibits the reverse procedure, as internal stops appear within all its
stanzas except the last, to parallel the speaker's change from scorn-
ful description of Bleaney's plight to the horrified admission that his
own may be worse. In "Wedding-Wind" and "Myxomatosis"
Larkin upsets regularity with a premature stanzaic split within the
line; his overloading the next stanza calls the reader's attention not
only to a shift in perspective from one stanza to the next, but to the
imperative nature of the viewpoint finally adopted.

Rhyme and meter constitute equally strategic sources of stanzaic
irregularity. "Reasons for Attendance" illustrates the full range of
Larkin's skills in imperfect rhyming by exhibiting an insistent off-
rhyme pattern even in the first stanza:

> The trumpet's voice, loud and authoritative,
> Draws me a moment to the lighted glass
> To watch the dancers—all under twenty-five—
> Shifting intently, face to flushed face,
> Solemnly on the beat of happiness.

Subsequent stanzas offer equally playful pairings—such as
sweat / what and here / share—which not only avoid the monotony
of strict rhyme, but correspond to the speaker's skeptical irony.
Only in the final stanza do the rhymes become perfect, and there
such regularity not only signals the poem's close, but sets up the
reader for the surprise reversal of the final line.

As a general principle, the more imperfect the rhyme scheme in a
Larkin poem, the more complex the viewpoint or the more reliable
the speaker. The reader should suspect the character in a perfectly
rhymed Larkin poem. In "Naturally the Foundation Will Pay Your

Expenses" perfect rhyme combines with stanzaic and metrical regularity to create a singsong effect indicating the shallowness of the academic world-traveler. Relatedly, the hapless speaker in "Self's the Man" develops his fairly naive position with much more exact rhyme than usually accorded to Larkin's speakers. And, though clearly exceptional in having both a very tight rhyme pattern and a wholly reliable speaker, "Going, Going" confirms Larkin's general practice by numerous internal pauses, end-stopped lines, and metrical irregularities which avoid the sense of simplemindedness arising from the other perfectly rhymed poems. Larkin often plays off one kind of regularity—rhyme, meter, or stanza / sentence—against another kind of irregularity, to support the sense of imperfection in life he would impart.

This contrast between subtlety and abrasiveness can operate within, as well as among, his poems. In "No Road" he uses caesurae, short second and final lines in each stanza, and feminine endings, to avoid strict iambic pentameter. Interestingly, he moves from the masculine endings of the rhymed couplet concluding his first stanza (neglect / effect), to feminine endings and weaker rhymes at the close of the second (longer / stronger), and finally to imperfect rhyme, as well as weak endings, in the last (fulfillment / ailment), while moving from a positive view of the past, through a neutral view of the present, and into a bleak view of the future. A reverse shift, from a looser to a tighter rhyme pattern, proves equally effective in the conclusions of "Born Yesterday" and "Arrivals, Departures" by helping reveal premises in the one and emphasizing a perplexing dilemma in the other.

In certain poems tension between metrical regularity and irregularity, or strategic deviation from a basic meter, constitutes an especially effective reinforcing device. While displaying an essentially iambic-pentameter line, "Maiden Name" departs frequently in its middle stanzas and especially in its final line—"with your depreciating luggage laden"—perhaps to undercut the confident manner with which the speaker purports to scorn his former friend. "Faith Healing" and "Home is so Sad" exhibit more strikingly strategic metrical irregularities. In the one poem key shifts in argument are signaled by sharp breaks in the iambic-pentameter scheme, while in the other departures from a similar pattern emphasize the finality of attitude being expressed. In "Wild Oats" we find extreme irregularity maintained until the final line, where a perfect iambic pattern not only marks the poem's end but reinforces

the caustic quality of the concluding statement, "Unlucky charms
perhaps." And in "How Distant," Larkin offers a series of four-line
stanzas with irregular line-length and meter except for the fourth
and fourteenth lines, where pairs of dactyls—"Rising and falling"
and "Ramifies endlessly"—help suggest the rocking of the sea, and
the final three lines, where iambic irregularity calls attention to the
striking conclusion by the speaker, as well as the witty images in
which it is cast:

> The huge decisions printed out by feet
> Inventing where they tread,
> The random windows conjuring a street.

Of course, these technical sources of stanzaic tension in Larkin's
poems are all accompanied by a full range of traditional rhetorical
devices. Such things as alliteration, repetition, parallelism, and an-
tithesis play key roles in many Larkin poems. While alliteration
reinforces a sense of closure in the final lines of "Next, Please" and
"Send No Money," in "Toads" it operates in the third and seventh
stanzas to help suggest the outlandishness of the speaker's
rationalizings. In the same poem Larkin marks a shift in his
character's thinking by repetition when he has him say:

> Ah, were I courageous enough
> To shout *Stuff your pension!*
> But I know, all too well, that's the stuff
> That dreams are made on.

Repetition figures prominently, too, in "MCMXIV," where the
repeated "never" in the final stanza adds dramatically to the sense
of totality in the break with Edwardian innocence, and in "Homage
to a Government," where Larkin jabs his reader with the repeated
phrases "Next year" and "all right" in understatedly expressing dissatisfaction with contemporary Britain's retreat from world power.
As for parallelism, he uses this to advantage in a number of poems,
usually to reinforce the mood of a particular ending.

Larkin's penchant for working irregularity against pattern, to
produce a technical tension in keeping with his ideological complexity, is perhaps no more forcefully revealed than in those few poems
designed around a traditional fixed sonnet form. In an early sonnet,
"Spring," he moves from the fairly regular iambic pentameter of
the first part to irregular meters and feminine ryhmes in the sestet,

to parallel the speaker's falling off in spirit. Likewise, in "Friday Night in the Royal Station Hotel," he implies a form combining elements of the Italian and Shakespearean sonnets, but deviates even from this—with numerous metrical irregularities, a split after the ninth line, and imperfect rhyme—while studiously avoiding any of the correspondence between syntax and divisions of the poem traditional to the sonnet. Finally, in "The Card Players" he supports the surreal quality of the picture he paints by undercutting the poem's tight rhyme scheme with numerous departures from iambic pentameter and pauses within lines, thus hiding his poem's resemblance to the traditional sonnet.

CHAPTER 6

Prose Writings

THUS far the discussion has focused largely upon Philip Larkin's accomplishments as a poet. Such a focus may cause one to forget that he has also authored two novels, one of which has been seen as an indicator of trends in postwar British fiction, a significant if limited body of literary essays and reviews in leading British periodicals, and several years of jazz columns sufficiently distinguished to warrant their being published as a collection. Larkin's excursions into editing, and particularly *The Oxford Book of Twentieth-Century English Verse,* have further marked him as both a spokesman and an influence in British literary taste.

I Jill

In his introduction to the revised edition of *Jill* (1964) Larkin asks for "the indulgence traditionally extended to juvenilia" and calls his first novel an "unambitious first story."[1] Even if we accept this appraisal, we need not deny *Jill* its singular charm or its important place in Larkin's development. In fact, if we consider the attempts at fiction by other distinguished poets—Cummings, Dylan Thomas, Sassoon, Plath, and Dickey, to name a few—*Jill* survives as a permanently readable and inherently interesting novel.

Its interest stems in part from the dilemma it describes, the dilemma of illusion and disillusionment shared with most of Larkin's better poems. The central figure of this dilemma, though, is a much younger version of the later Larkin characters, a first-year student named John Kemp, at Oxford at about the same time Larkin himself went there. Shy and self-conscious, the son of a retired policeman in Huddlesford, a town to the north of Oxford, Kemp finds himself sharing rooms with Christopher Warner, a brash, rich, and irresponsible Londoner. The novel recounts Kemp's first term, in which he struggles with the thoughtlessness of Warner

and his friends, with his own desperate desire to be accepted even
by those whose behavior increasingly strikes him as selfish and immature, and with the need to accomplish something academically
while wrestling with such personal uncertainties.

The means Kemp devises to cope with these pressures is a fantasy, or rather an outright lie which develops into a fantasy of independent fascination. After suffering weeks of exploitation by
Warner and his crowd—their opening Kemp's china and using it
even before he has arrived, Warner's borrowing from Kemp's
severely limited cash reserve seemingly without any intention of
repayment, Warner's cribbing from notes Kemp has conscientiously
collected for their common tutorials, and many other
humiliations—all to ingratiate himself with them, Kemp is over-
joyed at being asked by Christopher to meet his mother at the train
and to have tea with them. This triumph is soon destroyed, though,
when Kemp overhears Warner and his girl friend, Elizabeth, discussing him; he finds that Chris, Elizabeth, and Mrs. Warner all
consider him a spineless pawn. At this point Kemp angrily determines to invent something which will impress Christopher. Having
repeatedly imagined himself in other roles than his own—as Mrs.
Warner's son, as Christopher himself, and as his former
schoolmaster in Huddlesford—Kemp now imagines himself as an
older brother and invents a younger sister named Jill, from whom
he must concoct letters to entice the womanizing Warner.

Jill soon takes on a dimension beyond that originally intended for
her, however. She becomes a retreat for Kemp from his confusion in
the real world. Even while imagining her as a device to insure
Chris's interest, Kemp gives her a surname different from his own.
Very quickly he moves from letters to a fairly lengthy third-person
story in which he reworks the qualities and experiences already
assigned her in the letters. Then, dissatisfied with the story, he
moves to the diary-form. These frustrated attempts to give Jill a real
existence lead him to recognize the combination of qualities he has
given her in a girl he sees at a bookstore. Initially delighted at being
able to separate his fantasy world from reality, he has come increasingly to rue that separation; the sighting of a supposedly real
Jill logically concludes this increasing frustration.

Those parts of the book following this initial sighting concern
Kemp's amusing efforts to see the girl again and to find out who she
is. For some time she eludes him as he spends hours looking or
waiting for her in shops and eating places he believes she might

frequent. Anxious to keep Christopher away from her, whoever she is, he at last spots her and follows her to his own rooms, to discover that she is the cousin of Christopher's friend Elizabeth; fantasy and reality thus converge in cruelly ironic fashion. Refusing to be dismayed, however, Kemp volunteers to carry a message to Jill—or Gillian, her real name—and extracts from her a promise to meet him for tea in his rooms. His comic anticipation and elaborate preparations collapse, however, when Elizabeth shows up instead, to inform him that Gillian is much too young to be meeting him.

A few days later Kemp's intense disappointment is interrupted by the news that his hometown has been badly bombed. By visiting Huddlesford, to learn of his parents' fate, he finds a whole round of national and international crises just beyond the sheltered personal difficulties he has been facing at Oxford. His trip also reinforces the more realistic manner in which he appraises Christopher and his crowd once he returns to school.

But Jill proves not so easy to exorcise. Though Kemp disgustedly burns his Jill-writings, he seeks out Gillian at a party, where his drunkenly kissing her earns a punch from Christopher. Falling into a fountain as the result of this escapade, he suffers pneumonia, several days of unconsciousness, and a long spell in the hospital. Even there he dreams of rescuing Jill in some manner. While at the end of the novel Kemp has succeeded in throwing off the pernicious influence of Christopher, Jill remains a persistent if suppressed dream.

In all of this Kemp prefigures the characters of many Larkin poems. The effect of the novel rests upon a tension between comedy and serious disillusionment, a tension already noted as central to Larkin's poetry. We see in Kemp a youthful prototype of the rootlessness, fantasizing, rationalizing, and disillusionment characterizing individual poems from the two central collections. Here, as in the poetry, Larkin is both critical and sympathetic toward his principal figures. Kemp's concern for Christopher's approval is both pathetic and egocentric: if his desperation to please Warner reflects his want of self-confidence, his pride at being able to boast to people that he rooms with "the beastly Warner" reflects a consuming egoism deserving some sort of tumble. Likewise, the whole business of Jill can be seen both as a comic episode growing out of Kemp's immaturity and a potentially serious, if implicit, commentary on the relationship between at least one kind of literature and the reality from which it springs. Larkin almost has nature im-

itating art when Gillian arrives on the scene; in this we are reminded of his "Study of Reading Habits." Kemp's dejection when
Warner calls his self-sacrificing "white" resembles the speaker's
feelings in "Sympathy in White Major," just as his shyness toward
girls sets the pattern for most of the Larkin lovers.

Two minor characters in the novel likewise reflect attitudes central to Larkin's later writings. Kemp's only close Oxford associate
besides Christopher Warner is a fellow scholarship student named
Whitbread, whom he meets in the dining hall and visits periodically. As the novel develops, Kemp becomes increasingly torn between
the two men, neither of whom deserves his serious attention. If
Christopher is shallow, so is Whitbread, and perhaps in a more
reprehensible way. Though, unlike Warner, Whitbread takes his
studies seriously, he views academic matters in a crassly pragmatic
way. He cautions Kemp against stinginess because the dons might
regard him as a miser. He exhibits an almost embarrassing amount
of inside knowledge about other students, the dons, conditions in
the university, and the reputations of various preparatory schools.
And, he reproves Kemp for lacking the kind of push he manifests so
constantly.

Whitbread's aggressiveness is accompanied by decidedly poor
manners: repeatedly we see him handling or gorging his food, to
Kemp's annoyance. But, just as Kemp's lack of self-confidence
blinds him initially to Warner's weaknesses, it blinds him to Whitbread's. Larkin significantly includes a renunciation of Whitbread
in Kemp's later recognitions. The various jokes he finally plays on
Whitbread are every bit as important signs of his development as
his new response to Christopher or Elizabeth.

Whitbread exhibits the kind of shallow academicism generally
distrusted by Larkin. One reason he can initially impress Kemp is
that Kemp earlier has been encouraged by another proponent of
less than perfect academic ideals. His Huddlesford English master,
Joseph Crouch, took him under wing out of a sense of boredom;
though having little personal regard or intellectual respect for
Kemp, Crouch saw training his sixth-former for university entrance
exams as a challenging distraction. Essentially a worldling parading
as an academic, Crouch preaches to Kemp the virtues of a good
degree and the useful business contacts Oxford can bring. He looks
down on Kemp's lower-middle-class origins as much as would
Christopher Warner. Near the end of the novel, when he visits
Kemp at Oxford, it surprises only Kemp, and certainly not the

reader, to learn that Crouch has married and plans to join the air force. With characteristic practicality he comments that a service record will aid him in gaining good postwar employment, just as he warns Kemp against becoming a cloistered academic, lest he sacrifice the business career advantages which membership in even the dullest student organizations might bring.

Larkin seems to use Crouch both ways, suggesting the shallowness of his viewpoint even while applauding the honesty of his decision to forego schoolteaching for a world which, at least for Crouch, is more genuine. Larkin's debunking of Crouch's academic pose foreshadows "Posterity" and "Naturally the Foundation Will Bear Your Expenses," just as his treatment of Warner suggests the nonpolitical preference for the more common Englishman evident in most of his poems. Kemp interestingly regards his schoolmaster's final advice as well-intended but irrelevant. His inability to see it as superficial and perhaps insincere is a measure of his immaturity even after he has begun to question the objects of his once unquestioning allegiance.

II   A Girl In Winter

Larkin's second novel, published just a year later, has many obvious affinities to his first, and, like *Jill*, suggests both the kind of poetic outlook and technique he largely abandoned after *The North Ship* and the kind of poetry he was coming to regard as more genuinely his own. Again we see a young central character faced with discontinuity in his life, and we see Larkin developing the issues of disillusionment and self-realization in the maturing process he describes.

Like John Kemp, twenty-two-year-old Katherine Lind finds herself in an uncustomary setting, confronting people who treat her as a stranger. Unlike Kemp, she goes through no very painful period of trying to conform; rather, she has resolved not to be assimilated into her new surroundings. The reason for such a resolve, and its marked difference from Kemp's uncertainty, is that Katherine is literally a foreigner in England, a war refugee from an unspecified European country, and therefore subject to an isolation much more total than the class barriers disturbing Kemp. The main action of this later novel covers a single winter Saturday when Katherine, who has been in England for something more than a year and has gotten a library job in an unnamed provincial town, anticipates renewing the acquaintance of an English soldier whose home she visited several years earlier, when they were pen pals. Upon returning to England she has not reopened her correspondence with Robin Fennel or his family until noticing, a short time before the novel begins, a newspaper announcement that Robin's sister Jane had lost a young child. Sending her condolences to the family, Katherine learns that Robin may soon contact her; as the novel opens she is anticipating that reunion.

On this particular Saturday, though, her work routine is upset initially by a reprimand from her supervisor, Mr. Anstey, a mean-spirited tyrant who has advanced only because of wartime manpower exigencies and who does not hesitate to remind Katherine of her alien status. Hardly recovering from this unnerving confrontation, she agrees to accompany home Miss Green, a co-worker suffering a toothache. Having determined not to make friends in England or to entertain any personal involvement until returning to her home country at some distant time, she nevertheless is moved by the obvious dependence of the suffering Miss Green. She therefore takes Miss Green to a druggist, persuades her to visit a dentist, and even allows Miss Green to rest in her apartment. While there, she feels her emotional isolation further threatened by a note from Robin saying he will definitely visit her that day, probably before she finishes work.

Because of this feeling she leaves no note for him, a move she attempts repeatedly to justify to herself. After sending Miss Green back to work, she proceeds to return a purse she mistakenly picked up in the drugstore. By an improbable but morally appropriate coincidence, its owner turns out to be a Miss Veronica Parbury, who is considering a marriage offer from Anstey. Returning to work from Miss Parbury's rather late in the afternoon, Katherine suffers a second, more severe rebuff from Anstey, who gives her a telegraph message saying Robin cannot meet her after all. This time she retaliates by talking of resigning her position and, more effectively, by alluding to Miss Parbury. Leaving a shocked Anstey, she uneasily finishes her day's work and returns home, to find Robin camped at her door. The remaining chapters describe her attempts to resist Robin's advances while responding fairly and sympathetically to the dilemma of someone who, like herself, has had his life sharply interrupted by the war and who has difficulty envisioning any meaningful future. Robin ends up spending the night with her not because he can command deep feeling from Katherine, but because she can command an equanimity of which she is incapable when she first finds him. Though people and events seem to have conspired to upset her emotional balance, Larkin shows her finally at peace with herself and the outside world.

This description of the book's surface action scarcely accounts for its peaceful ending. Compared with *Jill*, *A Girl in Winter* concludes on a much more positive note regarding its central character's state of mind, because it ends with the final step of a fairly thoughtful process of self-examination by that character. Like John Kemp, Katherine falls prey to illusion and fantasizing, but in the end she understands much more fully where she has erred in perception and judgment. The final factor in her reaching this understanding is Robin's revelation that his sister Jane had named her child Katherine. Besides pleasing Katherine Lind, this bit of news adds to her reappraisal of the Fennel family and the time she spent with them.

Just as she had vowed to avoid any personal involvements upon returning to England, Katherine has striven to hold on to every remnant of her earlier life, hoping thus to bridge what she trusts will be a brief transition between that former life and reunion with her homeland. Such remnants include items of clothing which she insists on wearing, almost as badges to insure her alienation.

On the day in which the novel's main action occurs, she finds her resolve threatened from a number of sources. First, the possibility of a visit from Robin, which becomes imminent reality when she finds his note at her room, violates the tightness of the compartment to which she has relegated her relations with his family. Even before finding the note, she has developed mixed feelings about his visit. We see her repeatedly wondering what the Fennels would think of her library job; fearing a rebuff, she regrets having written them. Once Robin's visit becomes a certainty, she becomes more certainly apprehensive.

Yet, even as she suffers such apprehension, she begins to examine its basis. What she realizes, what the threat of the proposed visit forces her to realize, is that her three-week stay with the Fennels six years earlier represents the only unspoiled period of her past, and certainly a surer means of bridging the gap between past and future than clothes or other mementos subject to her continuing scrutiny and to time's destruction. Rather than risk spoiling the idealized memory of her relations with the Fennels, she has chosen, until recently, not to communicate even her return to England. But, having jeopardized the security of the relationship, she faces, in the coming meeting with Robin, precisely what she has feared most.

The nature and extent of her emotional investment in that dimly remembered holiday is made clear in the flashback center of the novel, where Larkin interrupts her present activities as she is about to return Miss Parbury's purse, to give a lengthy account of her earlier visit to England which contradicts most of her recollections. For one thing, though she remembers finding Robin Fennel a puzzle, she does remember finding him attractive. And, she remembers nothing at all about sister Jane. Her inability to remember either very distinctly Larkin renders ironic by showing the younger Katherine's feelings. As she first met Robin and his family she was quite attracted to him, finding him much more handsome than in his photograph and wondering when he would make romantic advances. His failure to do so made him puzzling to Katherine, who chose to believe that his generally polite and stiff behavior was but a covering for the "real" Robin. She imagined that he, too, was waiting for an opportunity for them to be alone so he could open up his feelings. When Jane remarked that "Robin is ordinary down to the last button," Katherine could only respond with disbelief, preferring to believe instead that he was quite extraordinary and that Jane was intent on squashing a likely romance.

Her suspicions about both of the younger Fennels collapsed when she learned that Jane herself had spurred Robin to invite Katherine to their home, hoping the foreigner would prove an interesting visitor to what Jane saw as her hopelessly dull situation. Katherine was immediately struck by the irony of her having snared the person she least wished to attract by her letters. Not even the kiss which Robin clumsily gave her the night before she left could draw her from this sense of irony. While they were at last alone, Jane herself received a marriage proposal from another of the family's guests, a development Larkin amusingly has Jane attribute to Katherine's tactfully having spirited Robin out of the way. Fully sensing the enormity of her misreading of others and of the egoism from which it sprang, Katherine vowed that never again would she be subject to romantic illusion.

All of this undercuts sharply her present view of that visit, to illustrate Larkin's contention, echoed throughout his poems, that human memory is extraordinarily selective and tends to romanticize the past in the face of an unromatic present. Faced with the rigors of wartime exile and loneliness, Katherine fears anything which might destroy the fragile edifice of imperfect recollection and fantasy composing her image of that summer with the Fennels. Larkin implies that she remembers perhaps better than she will admit, that the intrusion of Robin will uncover memories she has succeeded in drowning.

That she can deal with Robin ultimately in a calmer manner than such apprehension suggests is partly the result of her encounters with Miss Green and Miss Parbury earlier in the day. If Robin assaults what little is left of perfection in her past as she envisions it, the other two assault her present by making claims on the feelings and sympathies she has vowed to withhold. Moved to sympathetic action by Miss Green's dependence, she is even more struck by Miss Parbury's dilemma with Anstey. We learn that their relationship is complicated by Miss Parbury's invalid mother, whom Anstey has offered to support in a nursing home if Miss Parbury will marry him. But Miss Parbury indicates to Katherine that she cannot abandon her mother. Katherine is struck by Anstey's needing such a plain, simple woman as Miss Parbury, and by "the undertow of people's relations, two-thirds of which is without face with only begging and lonely hands" (p. 200).[2] She implicitly sees in this the paradigm for her relationship with the Fennels. Her recognition at this point prepares her to respond with empathy to Robin, as she can link his vulnerability with her own and with that of the others whose lives she has entered that day. So much have her feelings been aroused that she can even regret having thrown up Miss Parbury to Anstey.

Through her encounter with Robin she comes to deal realistically with her past and her present. Robin behaves very aggressively, at one point even raising the possibility of marriage. The difference between her response now and her anticipation six years earlier partly stems from the change in Robin, from a self-assured youth to an uncertain adult, but probably more from her having come to recognize fully the nature of her need in relation to him. Once such recognition is completed, she is superior to that need. And, once she has come to realize the more important need to fill her present and immediate future with meaningful living, however transitory, instead of unrealistically expecting a return to her past, she can respond to Robin not necessarily as a person she must love in any permanent sense, but as a person whose needs parallel her own and merit thoughtful concern.

Yet, such recognition is not really completed even when she

agrees to let him spend the night. Only the revelation about Jane's baby really completes it, as she recognizes at last her place in the Fennel family and the pitiful illusion of her which Jane must have harbored. Instead of nurturing such illusions herself, she now intends to explore the present and future for the happiness they might offer. Thus she can face the rest of her night with Robin, as well as tomorrow, with an openness and serenity markedly contrasting her earlier coldness and anxiety.

The prudence of facing reality squarely is an assumption *A Girl in Winter* shares with *Jill,* and with most of Larkin's mature writings. Significantly the two novels reflect much less sympathy with the human tendency toward illusion and fantasy than do the later poems. What Larkin as a poet has since treated as an understandable shying away from reality, as a novelist he treated as a principal source of irony. Significantly, too, the respective realities which the central characters of his novels try to avoid seem more bearable than the dead ends in which his later characters find themselves.

A Girl in Winter resembles *Jill,* too, in its bent toward realism. As in the earlier novel, Larkin here frequently loads a scene or character with realistic description. His various accounts of the streets through which Katherine walks, the library, and her apartment reflect such loading:

She looked from the unevenly-travelling bus, and saw a cheap dress shop, where a bare-ankled girl was arranging a copy of a stylish model; then a linen-draper's, with an old ceremonial frontage; a milk-bar, permanently blacked-out, with the door ajar and no-one on the tall stools; a pawn-shop window crowded with old coins, shirts, a theodolite, bed-pans and a harp; a public-house door with a bright brass rail, just opening; a sudden gap of high, papered walls and a heap of bricks, furred with frost, where a house had been destroyed. (p. 30)

Such a panoramic inventory reminds readers of various Larkin poems in which this technique is used, as do the descriptions of the fair at the Fennels' hometown during the novel's middle section.

Equally impressive in terms of realism is Larkin's lengthy rendering of Katherine's visit to the dentist with Miss Green, perhaps the most detailed account of such a visit in modern fiction. It begins with the outside corridor:

There was a sour smell here, as if the floors swabbed by the cleaner were never properly dry, and the woodwork was varnished a dark brown. The landing should have been lit by an inaccessible window, but this had been painted over with streaky black paint, and they had difficulty in seeing more than the outlines of things: the bannisters, a bucket of sand on the linoleum. Then they noticed a small board directing them into a poky corridor. They could hardly see. There were four doors in this corridor, with glass upper panels: two of them were blank. The others said, "waiting room" and "surgery." (p. 40)

The description of the surgery's interior follows the same tack, as does the behavior of Miss Green: "As she spat out the fragments of the filling she slobbered ludicrously, and was instantly self-conscious, trying to break the hanging thread by feeble shifting movements, searching for the handkerchief that was in her bag, and at last clumsily catching it away with her hand" (p. 44). All of the other details of the visit—such as the dirty elbows of the dentist's white coat, or his drill, with an "insidious" noise, which elongated "like an insect's legs"—reflect a sense of grim reality present throughout the novel. Significantly Larkin has the town waiting for a snow which refuses to come. The result is a sky in suspension which he describes in Hardyesque terms—"The sky remained as unmovable as a pebble frozen in the surface of a pond" (p. 177)—and a singularly unattractive scene on the ground: "It was not romantic or picturesque: the snow that was graceful in the country, was days old in the town: it had been trodden to a brown powder and shovelled into the gutters. Where it had not been disturbed, on burnt-out buildings, on warehouse roofs or sheds in the railway yards, it made the scene more dingy and dispirited" (p. 177).

To say, however, that the general viewpoint of A Girl in Winter is realistic in the same sense as Jill's is misleading, for the later novel clearly suggests a greater maturity of outlook and technique. In Jill realism operates as both an asset and a liability. Some readers, notably James Gindin, have taken the novel as a precursor to postwar fiction featuring a working-class hero,[3] provoking a denial by Larkin himself in the introduction to the second edition of Jill. Others have either complained of its excessive reliance upon realistic detail or praised it for succeeding despite its inherently realistic flavor.[4] Thus most readers seem to have taken Jill, whether a success or a failure, as largely realistic and in some ways suggestive of Lucky Jim and other Movement novels. Larkin's consternation suggests that he regards this view as mistaken.

Such a view, whether mistaken or not, is much less likely to arise with *A Girl in Winter*. There Larkin manages a much greater degree of perspective on his subject than is evident in *Jill* or any of the novels with which it has been compared. While *Jill* might be mistaken for autobiography, the female protagonist from a foreign country in the second novel largely prevents its being interpreted autobiographically. While Larkin undoubtedly drew heavily from his Wellington experience in writing this novel, ironically the only character whose position even approximates his at the Wellington Library is Anstey. The decided want of geographical specificity regarding the town and Katherine's home country adds to the universality of subject and action. In fact, Larkin deliberately blurs the issue of her nationality by implying that she comes from a nation invaded by an enemy of the British, by giving her an essentially Scandinavian name, yet by suggesting at one point that her home is near the Rhine. As in several of his later poems, Larkin uses the viewpoint of the outsider not for topical realism, but for perspective on certain qualities of English life and character; in this respect *A Girl in Winter* differs markedly from *Jill*. Another difference is that in general the narrator of *A Girl in Winter* comes off as more objective and less involved personally in the dilemma facing the protagonist, yet as somehow more sympathetic. Larkin conveys the impression of a central character whose crippling illusions are less immature and less unreasonable than those plaguing John Kemp. The disillusionment depicted in the later novel strikes the reader as much less amusing, as it stems from a basically serious, rather than comic, perspective in the narration.

A principal factor behind the greater universality and seriousness of *A Girl in Winter* is Larkin's use of images and concrete details in quasisymbolic fashion. As in most of his poems, such symbolic suggestiveness operates mostly unnoticed. Certainly this is true of the winter setting of the main narrative, compared with the high summer in which the flashback middle is set, which represents the contrast not only between schoolgirl joy and adult reality, but between Katherine's earlier openness and her more recent, self-enforced closeness of emotion. The beginning of a heavy snow at the very end of the novel signifies not only a welcome replacement for the bleak winter landscape noted earlier, but an emotional release into time and reality for Katherine herself. As in Larkin's poems, characters' responses to real concrete phenomena here suggest personality traits, as when the hopeless Jane Fennel searches the sky futilely for a rainbow, or when Katherine, in images suggestive of "MCMXIV," suddenly realizes the ephemerality of a popular song: "It was strange to think it had once sounded modern. Now it was like an awning propped in the sun nearly white, that years ago had been striped bright red and yellow" (p. 119). Through dozens of passages and scenes like this Larkin evokes the whole aura of time and human need characteristic of his best poems. The qualities of his narrative have prompted a critic recently to praise *A Girl in Winter* as "an astonishing *tour de force*, one of the finest and best sustained poems in the language,"[5] and to complain of its neglect. Certainly it merits more reading and more critical attention than it has received.

III *Criticism*

Philip Larkin's critical writings consist of slightly more than two dozen essays and reviews, plus his several years of monthly columns on jazz and jazz recordings. His literary criticism deals entirely with Victorian, Edwardian, and contemporary poets, his comments on the moderns dominating English poetry between the World Wars being contained in his criticism of their immediate predecessors and successors. Predictably, Larkin singles out Hardy and Betjeman for repeated attention, wondering at the failure of critics to appreciate Hardy's *Collected Poems* as "many times over the best body of poetic work this century so far has to show,"[6] and delighting in Betjeman's immense popularity. His remarks on more recent poets reflect the loyalties outlined in the earlier discussion of his poetic, while his sometimes elaborate reviews on the works and lives of such diverse figures as Rupert Brooke, Christina Rossetti, Wilfred Owen, Emily Dickinson, William Barnes, and Tennyson show his fascination with them not merely as verse technicians or representatives of the nineteenth and early twentieth centuries, but as personalities very near the surface of their poems. It is surely no coincidence that Larkin chooses to write mostly about very personal poets, for he is committed, as we have seen, to the idea of the poetic personality as an important factor in effective poetry.

Many of the other commitments reflected in his poems come through clearly in his criticism. Perhaps the chief of these is his commonsense insistence on clarity itself. Like his poems, his critical essays and reviews are written not for an exclusive, erudite clique, but for as broad a class of reasonably intelligent, but not necessarily scholarly, readers as possible. Further, each seems unwittingly designed to interest a reader perhaps unfamiliar with its subject, and most go beyond their stated concerns to draw conclusions at least indirectly touching the lives of most who would read them. Larkin tempers scholarship with common sense when discussing Hardy's poems about his dead wife or Housman's copy of the *Little Treasury* anthology:[7] these he relates to Hardy's strange reticence about his first marriage, or to the ways in which the forward-looking Housman, by the poems he deleted from his copy, appears the captive of Victorianism. It seems not unreasonable to see Larkin, writing an essay about the judgments accorded an anthology, rehearsing his own difficult choices encountered in preparing *The Oxford Book of Twentieth-Century English Verse*. Similarly, he insists on carrying over the inherent problem of a war poet like Wilfred Owen to our own times, to suggest the historical limitations necessarily attending Owen's viewpoint for most recent readers.[8] In each of these discussions Larkin proceeds with order and tact, quietly describing relevant circumstances and issues.

In fact, he implies in almost all of his literary criticism that a tentative validity is the most we can hope for when dealing with complex and frequently hidden matters of the human spirit. For this reason his efforts are often directed against the more absolute claims of others. He can share their puzzlement over the guilt expressed in Christina Rosetti's poems of the 1850s or the arrested development exhibited in most Emily Dickinson poems without accepting the various biographical conjectures most scholars would offer to solve these enticing puzzles.[9] Remarking that if hundreds of poems and letters have not made Miss Dickinson clear to us, it may be that she did not intend to be clear, and citing Hardy's extensive efforts to hide the truth about himself, Larkin seems almost content that those intentions should be respected and the mysteries surrounding them go unexplained, as if the mysteries themselves offer more fascinating testimony to the complexity and willfulness of human behavior than the explanations for them. As in many of his poems, Larkin suggests that the easy solution to a problem, scholarly or otherwise, may be merely tempting illusion, and that the more prudent course may be to recognize fully the dimensions of the problem and the impossibility of its absolute solution.

At the same time Larkin is determined to wrest what he can from a scholarly or biographical puzzle. If resistent to seemingly complete solutions, he does not hesitate to offer at least a modest interpretation, and one usually related to larger human concerns. Thus he sees in Hardy's strange inability to write of his love for his wife until their tortured life together was finished an impressive paradigm of the imperfection of all emotion, and in the "centrality of emotion" in Hardy's writings a celebration of truly human feelings.[10] Likewise, if he cannot accept Wilfred Owen's absolute pacifism as a realistic attitude in a world threatened by a Hitler or a Stalin, he nevertheless sees validity in Owen's insistence on the necessity of compassion, so much so that he praises Owen as "the only poet of this century after Hardy who can be read without a sense of bathos."[11] And, according to Larkin, if Tennyson must be criticized for frequent silliness and sentimentality, he must be credited with shrewdness and common sense in dealing with the most basic concerns and needs of man.[12] Because poetry for Larkin cannot be separated from life, criticism in his hands becomes a means of asserting that connection, of reminding us that true poems originate in the most personal feelings of their authors and touch the most personal feelings of their readers. All of this he insists with the sympathy and humor informing most of his own poetry.

His writings on jazz, the tenor of which has been suggested in connection with his poetic, operate in much the same manner. Of course, since he is obliged to discuss several recordings in a relatively short column, and since he must describe them to a more limited audience of jazz lovers, he is not so free to relate performances to performers' backgrounds. Nevertheless, such restrictions do not keep him from occasionally giving an enlivening biographical portrayal of a jazzman he especially admires, like Bechet, Pee Wee Russell, Armstrong, or Bessie Smith. Nor is he kept from devoting the bulk of a column to tangential questions like studio jazz, the economic plight of the jazz club musician, or the implications of the civil-rights movement for jazz. Consistently advocating a jazz of feeling and pleasure, he reserves his harsh comments for those displaying undue academicism or technical virtuosity at the expense of these larger principles—especially the saxophonist line of Charlie Parker, John Coltrane, and Ornette Coleman, by which Larkin traces the demise of the type of jazz he loves most. For a jazz enthusiast these columns are erudite, witty, and provocative. Even for a reader indifferent to jazz they offer a fascinating and amusing commentary on modern art and popular culture in England and the United States.

CHAPTER 7

Change and Growth

PHILIP Larkin has expressed admiration for Oscar Wilde's remark that "Only Mediocrities develop."[1] However, if he subscribes seriously to this view, he can take only limited comfort from his own writing career. One might argue, of course, that his novels prefigure not only the central concerns and assumptions of the poetry by which he is best known, or that the essentially "fictional" manner, the emphasis on character more than image which distinguishes his poems from the modernist poetry against which they react, continues in poems written some thirty years after *Jill*. However, even if one is unwilling to concede any substantial development from his novels to his mature poetry, a merely superficial examination of Larkin's first book of verse, *The North Ship*, suggests marked differences in attitude and technique from the later collections.

It suggests, too, his youthful confusion concerning the kinds of poetry he could write best, as well as the values he wished to impart in his verse, confusion which happily disappeared in the late 1940s and early 1950s, when he wrote those poems comprising *XX Poems* and *The Less Deceived*. Even if he is right in suspecting development as a sign of mediocrity, he must be pleased that his writing has developed away from *The North Ship*. And, though the poems in *High Windows*, his latest collection, much more closely resemble those of his two central collections than does almost anything in *The North Ship*—a resemblance signaled by the ease with which they have fit into the present discussion of Larkin's characteristic attitudes, situation, and techniques—they suggest, in perhaps subtler ways, that his development has continued and continues still.

I The North Ship *in Perspective*

No critic who has admired Larkin's poetry has expressed much satisfaction with *The North Ship*. Most of the poems in this earliest collection have been condemned as "juvenilia"[2] or as a carryover of "[what] the worst of Victorianism had carried over from the worst of Romanticism."[3] Even though most critics have welcomed the availability of these early poems, such has been the general distaste for all but a few, particularly in comparison with Larkin's later poetry, that Elizabeth Jenning's remark, "It is good to know that Larkin could write so well when still so young,"[4] appears an indeed exceptional response, if not a cryptic one. The more common view, and one supported by Larkin's introduction added for the 1967 revised edition, is that *The North Ship* poems reflect his youthful vulnerability to numerous influences—Yeats, Dylan Thomas, Keats, Tennyson, and others—before the example of Hardy helped him settle down to finding his own poetic voice. Though traces of such confusion and weakness remained in some of his later poems, the years immediately following *The North Ship* saw a fortunate, if gradual and painful, fusing of Larkin's instinct to write in a basically realistic vein, which he first realized in his fiction, with his need to write in more compressed forms, which he satisfied through lyric poems.

The North Ship anticipates his later work by dealing, however unsatisfactorily, with some subjects concerning him yet today. Then, as since, the majority of his poems show an isolated speaker painfully aware of his isolation. Although a much greater proportion of these early poems connect isolation and loneliness with love or its absence, we can see operating here the same assumptions about human relationships, namely their fragility and ephemerality, which occupy so much of his attention in the later collections. At the same time, Larkin early was offering the sense that relationships, however unsatisfactory, are more satisfying than isolation. And, in a few *North Ship* lyrics, such as "XXVIII" ("Is it for now or for always"), he extended his troubled perspective on love to ask the kind of metaphysical questions troubling his persona in dozens of later poems:

> Is it for now or for always,
> The world hangs on a stalk?
> Is it a trick or a trysting-place,
> The woods we have found to walk?

This suspicion of impermanence, which so clouds his vision of joy in his later writing, prevents him from viewing nature as benign.

Rather, as if anticipating "Sad Steps," he sees the bright moon as a perhaps malign force, "[having] drawn up / All quietness and certitude of worth . . . / . . . for they are gone from the earth" ("III"). Many other poems reflect the same negative response to the beauties of the dawn, the star-filled sky, or a woodland stream. In each instance Larkin refuses to advance an sentimentally optimistic view of nature. Nor is he unwilling to acknowledge death as the ultimate reality for nature and for man.

The problem, though, with almost all of the poems in *The North Ship* is that the view he is willing to advance appears sentimentally negative. If in terms of subjects, antiidealism, and humaneness, these poems prefigure his later writings, they fall far short of his later standards. In poem after poem the emotions expressed are vague and, in a real sense, premature. The Larkin speaker here comes off for the most part as emoting in a vacuum: while he may be responding to something actual, the poems fail to actualize that base of response. Repeatedly, as in the following examples, the reader is moved more by unsatisfied curiosity about why the character should be so miserable—mixed with some doubt that he actually is—than by sympathy at the depth of his misery:

> The moon is full tonight
> And hurts the eyes,
> It is so definite and bright.
> What if it has drawn up
> All quietness and certitude of worth
> Wherewith to fill its cup,
> Or mint a second moon, a paradise?—
> For they are gone from earth. ("III")

> If grief could burn out
> Like a sunken coal,
> The heart would rest quiet,
> The unrent soul
> Be still as a veil;
> But I have watched all night

> The fire grow silent,
> The grey ash soft:
> And I stir the stubborn flint
> The flames have left,
> And grief stirs, and the deft
> Heart lies impotent. ("XVIII")

> If hands could free you, heart,
>   Where would you fly?
> Far, beyond every part
> Of earth this running sky
> Makes desolate? Would you cross
> City and hill and sea,
>   If hands could set you free?
>
> I would not lift the latch;
>   For I could run
> Through fields, pit-valleys, catch
> All beauty under the sun—
> Still end in loss:
> I should find no bent arm, no bed
>   To rest my head. ("XXIII")

In another, longer poem ("II"—"This was your place of birth")
Larkin anticipates "The Building" by reflecting on a hospital and
by shifting from a neutral to a negative tone in his reflection. But,
where he entices the reader into "The Building" by making him
discover the poem's subject, in the earlier poem he attends largely
to himself and ignores his reader. He talks to himself, as the first
line suggests, and sets his negative reflections in the form of
questions to himself: "Are you prepared for what the night will
bring?" His heavy reliance upon conventional symbols and images—light / dark, day / night, and Death as "[t]he stranger who
will never show his face" or as an opponent in a card game—raises
the further question of whether, and how, the speaker knows what
he is talking about, in sharp contrast not only with "The Hospital,"
but with those more dramatic poems where Larkin characters muse
on death, such as "Mr. Bleaney" and "The Old Fools." Here a
definitely labored quality undermines the legitimacy of concern and
emotion.

Similarly the thirtieth selection in *The North Ship* ("So through
that unripe day you bore your head"), while resembling Hardy's
"Neutral Tones" in subject and point of view, differs in a way
which suggests characteristic weaknesses of the entire collection. As
in the Hardy poem, we have a character recalling the break-up of a
romance:

> So through that unripe day you bore your head,
> And the day was plucked and tasted bitter,
> As if still cold among the leaves.

Unlike Hardy, though, Larkin has his lover describe the break and their feelings on that occasion in no sharper terms than these:

> It was your severed image that grew sweeter,
> That floated, wing-stiff, focused in the sun
> Along uncertainty and gales of shame
> Blown out before I slept.

And, where Hardy's speaker draws the conclusion that love deceives, and grounds this conclusion in natural objects at the scene of his parting from his beloved, Larkin's inexplicably can draw no conclusion. Instead, he rails in rather petty fashion at his lost love, assuring her that his remembering is her "last, meticulous hour, / Cut, gummed; pastime of a provincial winter." As in most of the other *North Ship* poems, Larkin's speaker here does not approach the universal closely enough to deter us from wondering about his specific situation, yet he does not give us enough information about that situation and its antecedents for us to respond to him very clearly. As matters stand, we have neither a very complete character nor a very complete dilemma; what we are asked to respond to is merely a spurned lover's complaint, which, for all we can know, may just as likely be immature or unreasonable as mature or valid.

To be sure, the speaker in such poems may approximate Larkin at the time he wrote them, and very genuine personal circumstances may have prompted their composition. However, because the speaker can have no life outside the poems, and because Larkin gives him so little inside the poems, his feelings seem shallow and perhaps even unjustified. For what is the speaker grieving, why can he not celebrate the moon's beauty, or why does he regard his heart's plight as hopeless? These are questions the poems themselves raise, whether Larkin intended to raise them or not, and they are the type of questions to which in his later poetry he gives at least some satisfaction. Judging by his failure to answer them here, it must be concluded that he saw the power of these and most other *North Ship* poems resting somewhere other than in character and situation; since he gives so little of these, he apparently expected the reader's attention to be diverted to something else in the poems.

This intended source of poetic power seems to be the manner in which emotion is expressed, but it is there that the difficulties of thin characterization are compounded. The seeming shallowness of feeling put forth by these poems derives as much from the stock manner in which it is expressed as from deficient characterization. Not only do these poems tend to offer the commonplace romantic dilemma—a lover of some sort alone, amid either very unpleasant weather (windy, dark, rainy) or weather which for some unexplained reason he cannot acknowledge as pleasant—but his outpourings come in terms both formal and trite, suggesting a lack of spontaneity and sincerity, a greater attention by the speaker to his style than to his experience. Even those few poems, such as "XX" ("I see a girl dragged by the wrists"), where Larkin manages a measure of dramatic self-analysis, are weakened by the stage-quality of their diction. Lolette Kuby complains that in *The North Ship* "The poet poetizes; the poems advertise themselves as poems" and that even when the images are original they sound imitative.[5] All of this is in marked contrast not only with Larkin's later poems, but with the best of the English romantic tradition—the best of Wordsworth, Keats, Tennyson, and Yeats—out of which *The North Ship* attempts to rise. Timms points out how, despite Larkin's claim that Yeats was his master during the early 1940s, *The North Ship* poems totally lack the sexual vitality central to Yeat's love poems.[6] What we find instead, as the poems quoted earlier illustrate, is a reliance upon ill-defined stock materials, such as dreams and bad weather, couched in a mannered style.

A further problem in these poems is that they display little of the tension between stanza and sentence, or line and syntax, so enlivening Larkin's later verse. Where earlier he exploits the possibilities of prosodic regularity by playing it against irregularity, in *The North Ship* the poems seem unrelievedly regular, compounding the dullness induced by the problems of character and diction already noted. And yet, for all of their intended regularity, these early poems frequently contain lines not merely irregular or imperfect in meter or rhyme—not designed strategically, as in the later, more informal Larkin style—but rough and unpleasing:

> What beasts now hesitate,
> Clothed in cloudless air,
> In whom desire stands straight?
> What ploughman halts his pair
> To kick a broken plate
> Or coin turned up by the share?
> What lovers worry much
> That a ghost bids them touch? ("I")

Such a stanza as this makes the distinction between jerky and imperfect rhythm, a distinction of utmost importance in Larkin's
successful writing, readily apparent, as does the opening stanza of
"VII":

> The horns of the morning
> Are blowing, are shining,
> The meadows are bright
>   With the coldest dew;
> The dawn reassembles.
> Like the clash of gold cymbals
> The sky spreads its vans out
>   The sun hangs in view.

Here again we see a poem failing to live up to the principles of
regularity to which it is committed; rather than the pleasure or tension issuing from the irregularity in many later poems, we find
pointless distraction suggesting inpreciseness and error by the poet,
which, given the bardic quality Larkin seems to be aiming at in so
many of the *North Ship* lyrics, is ironically damaging.

Perhaps this bardic quality itself, or at least the tendency of the
Larkin speaker to take himself seriously at all times, constitutes the
gravest shortcoming of these poems. Nowhere in the entire volume,
even in those few poems which show promise of Larkin's better
writing to come, does the speaker take the ironic and humorous
perspective on himself or his situation so central to most of the later
poems. Repeatedly Larkin misses opportunities he would not
neglect later to involve his speaker in self-criticism and self-analysis,
which might distract the reader from questioning the speaker's
background; character could thus be illustrated, instead of being
left wanting.

Partly as the result of such unrelieved gravity, these poems display for the reader some confusion as to formal intention. While, as
we have seen, Larkin elsewhere creates poems mostly involving
either a character's situation or rhetorical assertions about life, here
we have poems of very vague intention, or at least of vague effect:
they fail to refer with sufficient specificity to the speaker's dilemma
to arouse feeling for him, yet they fail to move far enough beyond
him to qualify as assertions about life. Formally they lie in limbo. In
poem after poem we find open-ended complaining by the speaker,
prompting Kuby's contention that, with few exceptions, the poems

of *The North Ship* might just as well be viewed as "fragments of
one long plaintive sonata expressing budding disillusionment rather
than clearly separate poems." She sees the numbering of most
poems in the collection—sharply contrasting with the often pointed
titles of Larkin's later offerings—as symptomatic of this absence of
formal autonomy.[7] The speaker's constant cry—not about the
human condition we share with him, but about his unhappy state,
whatever it is—convinces us only of his egocentricity, and not of his
reliability or the validity of his complaints. Egocentricity, often the
object of comedy in Larkin's other collections, cancels out any sympathy in these poems, producing at best an emotional standoff and
at worst a degree of scorn certainly not intended by the poet.

II   *Developments in Maturity*

As has been suggested, *The North Ship* stands more by itself than
any of Larkin's other collections. The most striking and most permanent changes in his writing occurred in the years immediately
following World War II. Practically all of the selections in *XX
Poems* reflect these changes.

Subsequent developments are not so striking. One perhaps instructive way of charting Larkin's further changes as a poet in the
early 1950s is to compare selections from *XX Poems* which he chose
to omit from *The Less Deceived* with those he chose to retain, as
well as with new poems added for the later collection. Though it is
impossible, and perhaps irrelevant, to determine the basis for each
omission or retention, some interesting patterns emerge among the
three groups of poems. The dropping of "VII" ("Since the majority
of me") and the retaining of "XIII" ("Since we agreed to let the
road between us"), which became "No Roads" in *The Less Deceived,* perhaps reflects the poet's decision not to keep both poems dealing with basically the same ethical dilemma and working through
the device of the extended metaphor, as well as his preference for
the one with the more elaborate stanzaic and syntactic patterns.
And, as noted earlier, the dropping of "Oils" in favor of "Dry
Point" seems to represent Larkin's shift to a less romantic, more
critical view of sexuality. As many critics have pointed out, the
ninth selection of *XX Poems* ("Waiting for breakfast, while she
brushed her hair")—written in the late 1940s, omitted from *The
Less Deceived,* and revived for the 1966 edition of *The North
Ship*—suggests, by its specificity of character and image, just how

far Larkin had traveled from his early poetic style toward the poetry of his maturity.

Other retentions seem even more significant. "Latest Face" and "If, My Darling" constitute two of Larkin's early experiments with ironic or comic lyric speakers; even if the speaker in each is the poet, we nevertheless have the poet treating himself with perspective. The self-pitying lover of the earlier poems has, in these instances, been turned into a source of comic pleasure. Larkin's growing preference for a more ironic viewpoint in his lyrics may account for his leaving "Arrival" and "XV" ("Who called love conquering") out of his later book, for in each we find a plaintive speaker expressing his complaint in images reminiscent of the style Larkin had been trying to abandon for some time. The still-Yeatsian quality of these poems, as well as their self-pitying speakers, is contrasted even further in "Wedding-Wind" and "Deceptions," two others Larkin left in his collection. If the amusing lovers in "Latest Face" and "If, My Darling" can be associated with the poet, no such association is possible with the characters on whom Larkin turns his attention in these two poems: the bride of "Wedding-Wind" and the young girl of "Deceptions" seem creatures more of Larkin's imagination than of his personal experience—in neither poem do we sense the poet pitying himself.

As for setting, nature is shoved more to the background in the poems Larkin kept for *The Less Deceived;* even in the two retained poems dealing heavily with nature—"Coming" and "Spring"—he was careful to suggest an urban or town backdrop for his reflections. This note of urban, or at least technological, realism extends in some degree to all of the other retained poems. He employs it in "Next, Please," with its elaborate description of the ship; in "Wants," with its references to flagstaffs and life insurance; in "Wires," with its electric fences; and in "At Grass," with its numerous town references. These four poems signal, too, Larkin's growing commitment to a more universal level of implication in his verse, his having moved away from the purely, and perhaps selfishly, personal level. In general, his separating those poems he wished republished in what was to be his first critically acclaimed collection, from those he presumably preferred forgotten, reveals a turning away from the impulse merely to complain of discomfort, toward the impulse to define character and dilemma more objectively and with greater moral responsibility.

Certainly the other selections in *The Less Deceived,* which

Larkin wrote mostly between 1950 and 1954, confirm these impressions. "Places, Loved Ones," "Lines on a Young Lady's Photography Album," and "Reasons for Attendance" show a furtherance in his use of first-person speakers for complex effects, while "Church Going" represents his longest and most convincingly serious lyric up to that point in his career. His concern with ethical problems first revealed in *XX Poems* is combined with a greater felicity of imagery in such lyrics as "Whatever Happened?" and "Triple Time," while "I Remember, I Remember" and "Skin" extend the resources of his wit beyond their earlier achievement. And throughout *The Less Deceived* we see a greater variety of subjects, of characters, of tones, and of prosodic techniques than revealed even in the better of the *XX Poems*.

In many ways the poems in *The Whitsun Weddings* represent the full flowering of Larkin's poetic talents, the final casting off of his youthful misdirection. It was almost as if he had written a group of poems fully in line with his best writing in *The Less Deceived*. If not strikingly different from the immediately earlier collection, *The Whitsun Weddings* is notable in having a higher percentage of third-person poems, and of first-person poems with characters obviously not to be equated with Larkin himself. His bent toward realism, in characterization and setting, is evident in every one of these later poems, more so than in *The Less Deceived*.

For most readers, though, the poems of *The Less Deceived* blend into those of *The Whitsun Weddings;* we recognize these two books as Philip Larkin's central poetic achievement. His latest book, *High Windows*, clearly represents an extension of that achievement. With one or two exceptions, every one of these later poems recalls in some significant way an earlier poem by Larkin, which is why they fit so comfortably into a discussion of his characteristic attitudes and techniques. Nevertheless, some definite, if not surprising, trends away from *The Whitsun Weddings* period are evident here.

One of these is Larkin's greater bent in recent years toward contemporary topicality, both of subject and allusion. Perhaps this is a logical outcome of his steady development into realism. Where none of the *Less Deceived* poems addresses particular contemporary events, and where only "MCMXIV" among the *Whitsun Weddings* selections deals with public history, in *High Windows* we find two fairly long poems—"Going, Going" and "Homage to a Government"—dealing openly and solely with developments in contemporary Britain which distress Larkin, while a third selection,

"The Explosion," may refer to a particular castastrophe. And, while almost all of the remaining poems, in typical Larkin fashion, refer to the details of everyday life, two in particular, "Posterity" and "Annus Mirabilis," go far beyond his usual realism by depending largely upon such details for their effectiveness.

While "Posterity" resembles "Naturally the Foundation Will Pay Your Expenses" in that it satirizes academic phoniness, the more recent poem is much more caught up in the trivia of today: air-conditioning, academic tenure, Coke machines, Freshman Psych, jeans and sneakers. Of course, in the earlier satire, the speaker necessarily refers to more stable elements in British life. What is significant is that Larkin has his later academic, also a foreigner, reveal the emptiness of his position in such terms.

In a real sense, "Posterity" reflects Larkin's growing concern at the encroachment of American scholarship on British literature, a concern more elaborately expressed in his essay, "Operation Manuscript,"[8] where he urges the British to pay attention to the drain of British literary manuscripts to American libraries. This concern, of course, is only a part of his larger concern with the consequences of Britian losing her position of world leadership to the United States; the two nations' common language has permitted an especially speedy Americanization of British life since World War II. At any rate, this particular poem marks Larkin's first recognition in his poetry of this cultural takeover.

It marks, too, his first overt acknowledgment of his prominence as a poet, which makes him a likely target for Jake Balokowsky's treatment. Nowhere earlier has he appeared as a public figure, but only as a more or less common man facing the problems of existence common to us all. That in this first poetic recognition of his success he should have Jake, a young man, refer to him as an "old fart" suggests something besides the greater contemporaneity of *High Windows* compared with the earlier collections; it suggests the perspective of an admittedly older man. Though a hint of this perspective came in "Age" and "Dockery and Son," for the most part the reliable Larkin speaker—in poems like "Mr. Bleaney," "The Whitsun Weddings," and "Reference Back"—might be any age from his late twenties to well into middle age. Certainly he seems no older necessarily than Larkin's thoughtful churchgoer or the man outside the discotheque in "Reasons for Attendance."

In fact, a measure of the attractiveness of the speaker in such poems as these stems from the impression that he concerns himself

with such things as age and death long before he must. If the
speaker in *The North Ship* seems prematurely, and perhaps unnecessarily, sad, the speaker in most poems of the two central
collections seems prematurely wise in his reverence for questions
beyond his immediate or selfish concerns. In "Posterity," though,
and even more in "Annus Mirabilis," we find a combination of
topical reference—the end of the *Lady Chatterley* ban, the beginning of the Beatles, and perhaps the Profumo scandal—with the
perspective of a man for whom the sexual revolution has come "just
too late." This same open admission of middle age colors several
other poems—"High Windows," "Vers de Société," "Going,
Going," "Money," "Sympathy in White Major," and "Sad
Steps"—each of which gives the impression not simply of a man
who is choosing to live his life in a certain way, but who has lived
many years in that way. Where time and its pressures seem subjects
of independent fascination in earlier poems, here they strike him
more personally. Where earlier he looks toward the future, here he
confines his attention to either his past or his present, to render his
"We shall find out" at the end of "The Old Fools" more convincing
than had it been written earlier.

A consequence or corollary to the older perspective in *High Windows* is Larkin's greater identification with the speaker in his
poems, a reversal of his movement in the 1950s and early 1960s
toward greater dramatization and irony even in first-person poems.
Larkin comes closest to the self-deprecation of "Church Going,"
"Mr. Bleaney," or "Self's the Man" in "High Windows," where he
rehearses what he sees as a foolish response to the young.
Significantly, though, it is consciously a rehearsal, beginning with
"whenever." Where the speaker achieves wisdom only at the end of
those earlier poems, here he displays it from the beginning.

This is not to say that *High Windows* signifies any return to the
self-pity of *The North Ship*, reinforced by actual aging. On the contrary, the first-person character in these latest poems displays a
serenity owing to his wisdom and his awareness that his time is
limited. In retrospect self-pity appears the luxury of the young,
which is why in "Vers de Société" the speaker embraces social
events as a stay against self-pity, and why a poem like "High Windows" celebrates a stoic disavowal of simplistic envy for the young.
This wisdom, gathered through years of reflection, perhaps explains
what one reviewer has seen as Larkin's greater fascination in *High
Windows* with the value of habits and ritual.[9] Certainly poems like

"To the Sea" and "Show Saturday" demonstrate his deep respect for those events and practices linking individuals and generations despite the onslaught of time, an onslaught perhaps presented most forcibly in the ephemera of fashion and commercialism separating us in death and threatening to isolate us in life.

If the poetic self in *High Windows* is noticeably older than in Larkin's other books, it is not less creative. Perhaps the most startling thing about this last volume is its variety. Even though recalling others by him, each poem differs markedly from such predecessors, and in none of the earlier books has Larkin collected so many differing types of poems. This may be what one reviewer meant in remarking that there for the first time all of the Larkin motifs come together.[10] The central section of "Livings," for example, seems almost like many of the *North Ship* lyrics, but because it has a speaker obviously not Larkin himself, and because it is contained between two sections set in differing historical eras, it affords a much more vivid effect.

Likewise, "The Trees" might signal Larkin's return to his youthful preoccupation with nature, for it shows his awareness of the positive message of spring, coupled with an inability to accept that message. A consideration of the other poems of the *High Windows* period, plus a comparison of "Trees" not only with Larkin's early nature lyrics but with comparable poems from his middle volumes, reveals some interesting developments. As a nature poem "Trees" is unusual, if not unique, among Larkin's recent writings; "Cut Grass" and "Solar," the only other selections which might be placed in that category, display different ultimate intentions. Compared with the *North Ship* lyrics, however, there is more tension in "Trees," for the speaker engages in an analysis of nature's hold on man in springtime and an appreciation of its persistent recurrence. We have here not simply, as in so many of Larkin's early lyrics, an assertion of the speaker's misery even in nature—though such misery is an element operating in the poem—but an examination by the speaker resulting in his greater understanding of his relationship to nature. Even this slight growth in understanding is in sharp contrast with "Spring," its counterpart in *The Less Deceived*, where we see expressed only his painful awareness of alienation from spring's joy. "The Trees" differs, too, from his poem of the *Whitsun Weddings* period titled "Afternoons," which describes the terror of aging housewives, unable personally to share the optimism implicit in the cycles of nature. The line traced from this poem to "The Trees" illustrates Larkin's partial return to a more personal lyric outlook in recent years.

Of course, "The Trees" is but a mild indicator of the variety to be found in his latest collection. If some poems suggest his continuing realism, others display a nonrealistic or even surrealistic quality not usually associated with Larkin. Again there are precedents among his earlier poems. What strikes the reader familiar with those earlier efforts, though, is the more radical nature of at least one such recent poem. If earlier Larkin poems prepare us for the ending of "Solar":

> Coined there among
> Lonely horizontals
> You exist openly.
> Our seeds hourly
> Climb and return like angels.
> Enclosing like a hand,
> You give for ever.

or of "The Explosion":

> Plain as lettering in the chapels,
> It was said, and for a second
> Wives saw men of the explosion
> Larger than in life they managed—
> Gold as on a coin, or walking
> Somehow from the sun towards them,
> One showing the eggs unbroken.

nothing earlier prepares the reader for "The Card-Players":

> Jan van Hogspeuw staggers to the door
> And pisses at the dark. Outside, the rain
> Courses in cart-ruts down the deep mud lane.
> Inside, Dirk Dogstoerd pours himself some more,
> And holds a cinder to his clay with tongs,
> Belching out smoke. Old Prijck snores with the gale,
> His skull face firelit; someone behind drinks ale,
> And opens mussels, and croaks scraps of songs
> Towards the ham-hung rafters about love.
> Dirk deals the cards. Wet century-wide trees
> Clash in surrounding starlessness above
> This lamplit cave, where Jan turns back and farts,
> Gobs at the grate, and hits the queen of hearts.
>
> Rain, wind and fire! The secret, bestial peace!

In this verbal imitation of Dutch or Flemish genre painting, Larkin has extended the range of his wit to black humor, and revealed that element perhaps of despair, but certainly of cynicism, which may have lurked just behind his other humorous poems. As an interpretive allusion to all paintings with similar titles and subjects, this sonnet represents, for Larkin at least, a further means of weighing life, of showing the gap between reality and appearance, and perhaps of exploring the relationship between art and life. In projecting his viewpoint onto the stock materials of the genre painting, he has moved his poetry farther from concrete reality than before, and farther into the subconscious and nonrational. Perhaps more than any of his other recent poems, "The Card-Players" represents the kind of poem Larkin lately has wished to write, a kind not ordinarily associated with him. In this regard the whole of *High Windows* rewards his readers by reminding them of the range of his wit and talent sometimes forgotten by readers eager to praise or criticize his purely realistic writings. One can only trust that future poems and collections will continue to remind us of that range.

CHAPTER 8

Larkin, the Critics, and English Poetry

THE matter of appraising the work of a poet is perhaps neces- sary but necessarily difficult, particularly with a contemporary. Only slightly less difficult is the problem of determining his place in some sort of poetic tradition, as this too requires an objectivity not always possible with a living, developing writer, and involves the complication that the poetic tradition itself must be still evolving if any living writer can be said to fit into it. Both of these questions and possible answers to them invite the scorn of readers and writers alike, and become especially ironic with a poet like Philip Larkin, who has expressed such open and amusing skepticism about the conclusions reached by critics and literary historians. Certainly criticism and literary history represent, at best, imprecise and over- simplified versions of what poetry should be and has been. Certain- ly, too, one must take the pronouncements of critics and historians with these limitations in mind.

I Appraisal

A brief survey of Larkin's reputation among critics does nothing to dispel one's sense of such limitations. Critical commentary since the publication of *The Less Deceived* represents a full range of ap- praisals, from condemnation to high praise, and a range of bases for criticism. Larkin's detractors for the most part have shown a nostalgic regret for the demise of modernism in mid-century British verse. One suspects that even before Larkin became known, possibly even before that notable *Spectator* article introduced the term "Movement," many critics had formulated a marked distaste for those Movement writers they already knew; though relatively a latecomer, Larkin proved no puzzle to those bent, apparently, upon placing the nonmodernist poets into the "Movement" bag, even at the price of overlooking elements and qualities largely peculiar to the individual writer or totally unrelated to the modernism / Movement dispute.

While several critics on both sides of the Atlantic have consistently written more or less hostile criticism of Larkin's verse, perhaps the most consistently and most insistently hostile has been M. L. Rosenthal, who has known and commented on Larkin's poetry since the 1950s. In a review of *The Less Deceived* upon its initial American publication, Rosenthal saw Larkin as a representative of "the younger group of self-snubbers and self-loathers . . . who have recently risen to the fore in English letters," and went on to complain of the self-pitying egomania and petty bitterness reflected in his poems.[1] A more recent statement by the same critic on the same poet reveals Rosenthal's continued belief that a "fundamental lugubriousness" mars most of Larkin's writing; he sees in Larkin's "colloquial ease and half-confessional naturalness" only thin disguises for the question-begging inherent in his dreary view of life.[2]

Rosenthal's viewpoint has been expounded by numerous others, such as Colin Falck, who, if willing to concede that Larkin captures the feel of life for many ordinary people, nevertheless insists that he has done this "only at the expense of a deeper and more important humanity . . . ultimately at the expense of poetry,"[3] and Donald Hall, who predicts that Larkin soon will become "a small figure in the shadow of Hardy."[4] The regret of many critics that Larkin has not proven more affirmative or at least less prosaic in his choice of subjects, his attitudes, and his diction and verse techniques has even taken the form of a complaint that Larkin especially has misled American readers, indeed poetry lovers throughout the world, into believing that modernism and experimentation are dead in Britain. "There *is* a contemporary British poetry which is modern," one recent anthologist has declared: "Too often 'British' means *old* or *tired* in America, 'contemporary' rather than 'modern,' Philip Larkin rather than Tom Raworth."[5]

Of course, besides such disfavor Larkin in the last twenty years has enjoyed much critical favor. Just as he shared, perhaps undeservedly, the attacks made on Movement writing, he shared, also perhaps undeservedly, the acclaim given Movement writers as a group. Only as the many young writers of the 1950s have developed in distinctive directions and as terms like "The Movement" and "Angry Young Men" have disappeared from usage has it become possible for readers and critics to appreciate very fully the characteristic strengths and limitations of his poetry.

After reading Larkin for over two decades, some critics, among them distinguished poets, see him as England's finest poet. Donald Davie calls Larkin both "the central figure in British poetry over the last twenty years" and "the effective unofficial laureate of post-1945 England,"[6] labels which John Press, another prominent poet, has heartily endorsed.[7] In the same vein Calvin Bedient has called Larkin "the *other* English Poet Laureate, even more loved and needed than the official one, John Betjeman,"[8] while Clive James has looked back on Larkin's four thin collections in thirty years and concluded, "Not exactly a torrent of creativity: just the best."[9]

The defense of Larkin, like the attack, has centered on the issues of poetic technique, subject-matter, and attitude. Where negative critics like Rosenthal might complain of the drearily prosaic quality of Larkin's writing and of his failure to strike out on an original and demonstrably "poetic" course, his defenders usually turn this into a virtue by suggesting that his is a technique and style which, because it is not flashy, causes reader and critic to underrate its craftsmanship. The sense of orderliness in almost every one of his poems, which the promodernist would see as confining and dull, many readers in England and America have praised as an ultimate refinement. Thus Louis Martz says of Larkin: "He draws together in his work the qualities of the intellectual tradition in modern poetry; witty, analytic, metaphysical, and meditative, he brings that great tradition to a pause."[10] Similarly Calvin Bedient points out that, whatever the impression given by its nonchalant style, "A Larkin poem does not just happen; it is as concentrated as heart surgery."[11]

As for the subjects of the poems, which many have found too trivial and restricting, again Larkin's defenders insist upon their propriety, indeed their necessity in today's world. Lolette Kuby defends him against the charge that he shies away from the "big" subjects and against the corollary charges of egocentricity and self-pity by insisting that because in the twentieth century public life has become inescapably internal, Larkin's poems seem more appropriate to the age even than *The Waste Land*.[12] Likewise Kingsley Amis applauds the seemingly trivial base from which so many Larkin poems spring; the poems, like life itself, sneak up on the reader through seemingly unedifying details. It is this apparent unimportance of subject and detail which, according to Amis, makes the poems emotionally and morally authentic.[13]

The tone and attitude taken by Larkin in most of his poems have also been roundly defended. Where some critics have attacked his "dismissal of the world" for its negativism, Calvin Bedient insists upon distinguishing Larkin from other nihilists. While viewing Larkin as "unillusioned, with a metaphysical zero in his bones," Bedient claims that Larkin's dismissal itself is a "proud, self-affirming act," a model response. Because Larkin can find poetry and humor in an admittedly sterile world, he shows his readers a gentle and graceful way of coping with reality, an alternative to both romantic denial and nihilistic despair.[14] In part this is why Donald Davie attributes an "extreme humanism" to Larkin's tolerance of the ugliness in contemporary England: "Larkin . . . agrees to tolerate the intolerable for the sake of human solidarity with those who don't find it intolerable at all."[15]

As for the effective appeal of Larkin's rarely joyful outlook, the comments of at least one fellow-poet, Ted Hughes, offer his defenders impressive ammunition. Hughes, with whom Larkin has been compared both favorably and unfavorably, confesses, "All Larkin's poems are sad, and I like them all, but the sadder they are the more I like them"[16]—this from a writer who, most readers would agree, does not write at all like Larkin and who has been hailed by critics hostile to Larkin for having moved in the experimental direction in which they feel all British poetry ought to be moving.

Of course, much of the praise meted out to Larkin has been qualified. Some critics have seen both his strengths and his weaknesses, without drawing any final valuation. One such critic has praised Larkin for his honesty while noting a sort of "little Englandism" in his narrowly conceived subjects.[17] Another has suggested that Larkin's "offhand, debunking stance" may offset this narrowness and possible self-pity emerging from many of the poems, without concluding that it actually succeeds in doing so.[18] And a third "neutral" critic, perhaps summing up the attitudes of all the others, borrows Arnold's comment on Thomas Gray—"He is the scantest and frailest of classics in our poetry, but he is a classic"—and Faulkner's purported remark on Hemingway—"One would like to see some courage"—to express his own qualified admiration for Larkin's poetic achievement.[19]

While such criticisms as these—hostile, enthusiastic, and guarded—may suggest the futility of criticism, they should suggest that Philip Larkin has inspired a lively, if not always enlightened, debate. Because his detractors have said probably the worst things which could be said about him as a poet, and because his defenders have said probably the best, it becomes difficult to add anything by way of critical comment. The sometimes vehement remarks from both camps suggest the need for the kind of critical pluralism recommended some time ago by R. S. Crane, a recognition that a poet or poem is not simply good or bad in an absolute sense, but in relation to some particular focus: the formal tightness of specific poems, their "truth" in relation to the outside world or to life in general, or the effectiveness of rhetorical and poetic devices employed by the poet, to mention but a few possibilities.[20] Each of these represents a distinct area of concern for the critic; no one of them represents sufficient cause for wholesale praise or condemnation. Because so few of Larkin's critics, even when they recognize bases for criticism other than their own, seem willing to admit that each basis is equally important for a total evaluation of his work, and insist instead on concluding that he is a "good" or "bad" poet in an absolute sense, Larkin has scarcely received the kind of critical treatment his poems merit.

The absolutist criticism given his poetry suggests that he has been the victim of critics unwilling to appreciate the peculiar intentions of individual poems and to measure such poems against those intentions, instead of imposing their own biases on poems and a poet which they may never fit. It is perhaps impatience with this sort of approach which has prompted at least one Larkin critic recently to go on the offensive. Reviewing *High Windows*, Clive James has admitted Larkin's limitations yet insisted that "Without the limitations there would be no Larkin—the beam cuts *because* it's narrow":

[Among many critics] there is always the suggestion that Larkin might handle his talent better if he were a more well-rounded character. That Larkin's gift might be part and parcel of his own peculiar nature isn't a question they have felt called upon to deal with. . . . It ought to be obvious that Larkin is not a universal poet in the thematic sense—in fact, he is a self-proclaimed stranger to a good half, *the* good half of life. You wonder what a critic who complains of this imagines he is praising when he allows that Larkin is still pretty good anyway, perhaps even great. What's missing in Larkin doesn't just tend to be missing, it's glaringly, achingly, unarguably *missing*. But the poetry is all there.[21]

James's remarks suggests, of course, his own peculiar focus—he is less concerned, in a critical sense, with positive vision than he is with "poetry"—but they rightly suggest the need for critics sometime to assess Larkin's poetry on its own terms and to see such an assessment as at least as significant as what they would engage in. For, were they to practice a more pluralistic criticism on Larkin, they might conclude that he is both great and not-so-great, or both bad and not-so-bad, without appearing self-contradictory or absurd.

II *Placement*

The hostility expressed toward Larkin's poetry reflects very much the stage in English literary history in which he has lived and written, and his place in that history. It reflects, too, an inherent problem in the kind of poetry he writes, a problem he anticipated in a poem written in the 1940s:

> Words as plain as hen-birds' wings
> Do not lie,
> Do not over-broider things—
> Are too shy.
>
> Thoughts that shuffle round like pence
> Through each reign,
> Wear down to their simplest sense,
> Yet remain.
>
> Weeds are not supposed to grow,
> But by degrees
> Some achieve a flower, although
> No one sees. ("Modesties")

"Plain" words and "shuffling" thoughts rarely attract much attention; compared with their flashier counterparts, they always appear to make what one of Larkin's critics has called "the quiet poem."[22]

Of course, Larkin's special form of modesty and quietness emerged at the time when the other so-called Movement writers had begun a public revolt against the excesses of Modernism. His being taken by many as necessarily a part of that revolt was both fair and unfair, both accurate and inaccurate. As we have seen, the broad outlines of his theory of art and poetry coincide with that of the Movement position. However, as many of his admirers have rightly insisted, in practice he differs markedly from almost all of his contemporaries with whom he has been grouped. Just as most of his detractors attribute to him the deficiencies of the other Movement poets, his admirers have tended to emphasize the differences between him and the others, and to judge his work as superior to theirs.

If emotional detachment is a hallmark of Movement writing—and for many British writers emerging in the 1950s it was—then Larkin has never measured up to that standard.[23] Even in his mature revolt against the romantic excesses of his early poetry there has continued to be not just emotion, but understanding and compassion for the emotions of others. In this he differs from Kingsley Amis; though Amis can match Larkin's humor, Larkin reveals in his verse a much greater tolerance for human weakness, a much greater tendency to pity the weak and erring even while exposing their errors, than Amis has ever shown in either his verse or his fiction. And, while the clarity of Larkin's poems equals that of Donald Davie, a Movement poet known for his outspoken insistence on "purity" in English poetic diction and the other poet besides Larkin said to have clearly outstripped his Movement contemporaries, Larkin's range of tone and feeling—his wit, as well as his sympathy—far surpasses Davie's.

Beside Larkin's writing, most of Davie's seems stiff and hopelessly academic, while that of Amis seems flippant. One can imagine, for example, what *Lucky Jim* would be like had Larkin written it: certainly different from *Jill*, but certainly different from Amis's novel, since by the mid-1950s Larkin was well into writing poems—like "Lines on a Young Lady's Photograph Album," "Latest Face," or "I Remember, I Remember"—in which seriousness is balanced by humor, and derision is tempered by patience and affection. Comparing Larkin with Davie or Amis suggests how much wider was the range of his talents even when there seemed to be a Movement to which they all belonged. His poems since then only reinforce our sense of how much more difficult Larkin is to categorize in this way than almost all of the other Movement poets.

As for his place in the larger English poetic tradition, this is perhaps easier to determine, though again we must remember that period labels and movements in earlier centuries are probably no more accurate than those developed in this century; as time has passed it has simply become increasingly difficult to loosen their hold on us or to undo the mischief they have caused. Thus, while we can trace Larkin's descent back to Ben Jonson, through the

Augustans, Wordsworth, George Eliot, and Hardy,[24] we must remember that their writings, like his, displayed peculiar features resistent to categorization and that such tracing tends to blur their characteristic qualities as writers and literary personalities, which are probably the real reasons why they have remained great and readable. Certainly Larkin favors clarity, honesty, and reason in his verse, in contrast with many of his contemporaries, but he does not favor these at the expense of his feelings for the plight of man in the twentieth century any more than Eliot, Pope, or Jonson wished to dispense with such feelings in their centuries. The comparison of Larkin with Wordsworth and George Eliot, which has been endorsed repeatedly in this study, suggests his—and perhaps their—oblique relationship to the Romantic Movement, with which he is usually disassociated. What he shares with all of the earlier authors with whom he has been linked is not dispassionateness *per se*, but a distrust of excessive emotion and excessive rationality. To the extent that Pope and Jonson have been considered coldly rational, they have been misjudged; their affinities with Philip Larkin should suggest the extent of such misjudgment.

The difficulty of locating Larkin by means of period labels becomes especially pronounced when relating him to the established writers of this century. His opposition to the modernist position has been discussed; in this he can be linked with Robert Frost, Robert Graves, and George Orwell. However, his distaste for modernism does not make him an enemy of the major voices in British literature usually claimed by the extreme modernists as their own. Nor does it make him simply a throwback to an earlier way of writing or looking at life.

The range of Larkin's concerns and practices as a poet fully qualifies him as a participant in the intense and often anxious dialogue informing British literature since World War I. For all of his affection for English traditions—literary, moral, social, and religious—he projects in dozens of poems the recognition that man can no longer live by these, that he must face the sad reality of a largely rootless twentieth century. In this sensing of England's radical crisis, Larkin stands with Yeats, Lawrence, Eliot, and most other important voices in modern British literature. Like them, he recognizes that the issue of man's relationship to his past, to some sort of tradition, has become critical in an age wary of those traditions and institutions which directed behavior in the nineteenth century. The same impulse which guided Yeats in his search for an authentically Irish past and in his later mythological constructions, and which guided Eliot in his embrace of the older Ango-Catholic tradition, has guided Larkin in the writing of most of his poems. He, too, sees the various revolutions of the present century as both beneficial and harmful: beneficial in allowing the possibility of a more realistic appraisal of life, but harmful in risking the obliteration of that healthy strain of continuity essential to our well-being. Thus Larkin can sympathize with the religious urgings of a T. S. Eliot even if he cannot accept Eliot's religious solution to modern man's dilemma. And, because he shares a sort of tangential Platonism with Yeats, the dream-myth of Byzantium, at least in its general outline, would hold much attraction for Larkin's characters.

Realism connects Larkin not only with Eliot's "Wasteland" portrayal of modern existence, or Yeats's insistence on the significance and beauty of the physical and the concrete, as in the Crazy Jane poems, but most especially with D. H. Lawrence, who probably represents for Larkin the most direct twentieth-century link with the Wordsworth tradition. A distrust of attitudes derived from purely academic experience, an awareness of the limits of rationality, a care for the distinction between sentiment and sentimentality, and an honesty of observation are all strains central to Larkin's way of writing which mark his affinity with Lawrence. Even Lawrence's celebrated denial of traditional characterization finds its parallel in the Larkin speaker who in most cases reaches a stalemate in attempting to choose between conflicting pressures and attractions. Irving Howe's description of the "modern" Lawrentian hero as a "man divided between the absolutism of his individuality and the frustration of his societal instinct"[25] surely fits the speakers in "Dockery and Son," "High Windows," "Church Going," and many other Larkin poems. While Larkin cannot subscribe to the answers ultimately proposed by Lawrence, his poems represent more recent attempts to deal with many of the same problems and with the same candor which are his legacy from Lawrence.

It might, in fact, be argued that in Philip Larkin we see most of the often conflicting impulses of modern British literature converging, and that his treating them with a pecularily postwar perspective unavailable to the earlier moderns constitutes his distinctive contribution to English literature in the twentieth century. He thus becomes essential to the modern period, as he holds together those concerns and values which connected major British writers between the two world wars much more strongly than did any radical literary stance often imputed to them. It may be that Lawrence, Yeats, Eliot, Auden, and even Dylan Thomas no more "belonged" to Modernism than Larkin belonged to The Movement. Certainly his complaint seems to rest more with those critics and academics who have dehumanized the principal modern authors than with the authors themselves. In attacking James Joyce as representative of literary Modernism, Larkin may really, if perhaps unwittingly, be attacking the extreme Joyceans; at least one strain of commentary on Joyce and his writings suggests that Joyce and Larkin have much more in common, in terms of humane concern for the problems and details of everyday life, than modernist critics have allowed.[26] And, if Pound represents an extreme unacceptable to Larkin, he seems extreme in comparison with the other moderns, as well, provoking a measure of dissent in their practices as poets and novelists. Larkin's quarrel, then, is more with the doctrinaire theorists and imitators of Modernism than with the modern writers themselves.

His affinity with other principal British poets and novelists of this century stems from their shared attempt to reconcile elements of various traditions in British life and literature—notably romanticism, neo-classicism, and Christianity—with the realities of contemporary existence. His most recent poems suggest the most recent stage of his ongoing search for a version of the modern with which he can live comfortably. If his verse techniques, his choice of specific characters and situations, or the descriptive details of his poems betray a persistent regret that the old ways are largely gone or insufficient for life today, they also suggest that indeed such things are insufficient and that each of us must find in himself the means not so much of overcoming reality—this seems to be what many modernists would offer—as assessing and accepting reality with tact and grace. Larkin's poems suggest not reckless schemes for dealing with an ugly world—he would not presume to tell us what to do—but a state of mind in which a measure of serenity and love can accrue.

The impatience of many critics with so limited a formula—which stresses survival, rather than prosperity—may reflect their impatience with modern life, but it does not alter the nature of that life or refute the validity of Larkin's stance. Recent history offers numerous instances of the terrible price to be paid for collective extremes of both emotion and reason, and suggest that such recklessness is a luxury mankind can no longer afford. In his tacit assumption that the present century differs from its predecessors, Philip Larkin may resemble the advocates of radical modernism more than they or he would care to admit. But, in his quiet insistence that we preserve what we can, but only what we can, of our personal and collective pasts, while cultivating the resources for dealing sensibily with the individual and collective uncertainties of the future, he is surely more humane.

Notes and References

Preface

1. Philip Larkin, *High Windows* (New York: Farrar, Straus and Giroux, 1975).
2. David Timms, *Philip Larkin* (New York: Barnes and Noble, 1973); Lolette B. Kuby, *An Uncommon Poet for the Common Man. A Study of Philip Larkin's Poetry* (The Hague: Mouton, 1974).

Chapter One

1. Philip Larkin, "Not the Place's Fault," *Umbrella*, 1 (Summer 1959), p. 109.
2. *Ibid.*, p. 110.
3. *Ibid.*, p. 111.
4. Timms, *Philip Larkin*, p. 4.
5. See his recorded comments on "For Sidney Bechet," included in his 1964 recorded reading and commentary on poems in *The Whitsun Weddings*, produced by The Marvell Press.
6. Quoted in John Horder, "Poet on the 8.15," *Manchester Guardian*, 20 May 1965, p. 9.
7. Timms, *Philip Larkin*, p. 4.
8. Philip Larkin, "Introduction" to *Jill*, 2nd ed. (London: Faber and Faber, 1964), pp. 11 - 12.
9. *Ibid.*, p. 12.
10. *Ibid.*, p. 13.
11. *Ibid.*, p. 15.
12. Horder, "Poet on the 8.15," p. 9.
13. Douglas Oliver, "Poet Who Captures the Music of Daily Life," *Coventry Evening Telegraph*, 6 October 1972, p. 30.
14. "Introduction" to 2nd ed. of *Jill*, p. 19.
15. Philip Larkin, "Introduction" to *The North Ship*, 2nd ed. (London: Faber and Faber, 1966), p. 10.
16. *Ibid.*
17. Francis Hill, "A Sharp-Edged View," *Times Educational Supplement*, 19 May 1972, p. 19.
18. "Four Young Poets—I: Philip Larkin," *Times Educational Supplement*, 13 July 1956, p. 933.
19. Hill, "A Sharp-Edged View," p. 19.

20. *Ibid.*

21. Judith Anne Johnson, "The Development of Philip Larkin's Poetry," Unpublished Master's dissertation (North Dakota State University of Agriculture and Applied Science, Fargo, 1965), p. 29.

22. Larkin, "Not the Place's Fault," p. 111.

Chapter Two

1. G. S. Fraser, *Vision and Rhetoric: Studies in Modern Poetry* (London: Faber and Faber, 1959), p. 262.

2. Anthony Thwaite, "The Poetry of Philip Larkin," in *The Survival of Poetry: A Contemporary Survey*, ed. Martin Dodsworth (London: Faber and Faber, 1970), p. 43.

3. Philip Larkin, *All What Jazz. A Record Diary, 1961 - 68* (New York: St. Martin's Press, 1970), p. 17.

4. *Ibid.*, p. 96.

5. *Ibid.*, pp. 11 - 12.

6. *Ibid.*, p. 12.

7. "The Writer in His Age: Philip Larkin," *London Magazine*, 4 (May 1957), p. 47.

8. Philip Larkin, "The Pleasure Principle," *Listen*, 2 (Summer-Autumn 1957), p. 28.

9. Philip Larkin, "Betjeman en Bloc," *Listen*, 3 (Spring 1959), p. 15.

10. Larkin, "The Pleasure Principle," p. 28.

11. *Ibid.*, p. 29.

12. Thwaite, "The Poetry of Philip Larkin," p. 47.

13. Larkin, "Betjeman en Bloc," p. 15.

14. Larkin, "The Pleasure Principle," p. 31.

15. "In the Movement," *Spectator*, 193 (1 October 1954), pp. 399 - 400.

16. Robert Conquest, "Introduction" to *New Lines* (London: Macmillan & Co., 1956), p. xvi.

17. *Ibid.*, p. xv.

18. Derek Stanford, "Report from London—Literature in England: The Present Position," *Western Review*, 21 (Spring 1957), pp. 294 - 95; Bernard Bergonzi, "After 'The Movement,'" *The Listener*, 66 (August 24, 1961), pp. 284 - 85.

19. Leslie Fiedler, "Class War in British Literature," *Esquire*, 49 (April 1958), p. 80.

Chapter Three

1. Philip Gardner, "The Wintry Drum: The Poetry of Philip Larkin," *Dalhousie Review*, 48 (Spring 1968), p. 91.

2. A. Kingsley Weatherhead, "Philip Larkin of England," *ELH*, 38 (December 1971), p. 617.

3. *All What Jazz*, p. 18.

4. See his recording of *The Whitsun Weddings*.
5. *Ibid.*
6. Fiedler, "Class War in British Literature," p. 80.
7. See his recording of *The Whitsun Weddings*.
8. *Ibid.*
9. Lolette B. Kuby, *An Uncommon Poet for the Common Man*. p. 108.
10. *Ibid.*, p. 105.
11. *Ibid.*
12. *Ibid.*, p. 183.
13. *Ibid.*, p. 23.
14. See his recording of *The Whitsun Weddings*.
15. Calvin Bedient, *Eight Contemporary Poets* (London: Oxford University Press, 1974), p. 69.
16. Martin Dodsworth, "The Climate of Pain in Recent Poetry," *London Magazine*, n.s. 4 (November 1964), p. 91.
17. A. Kingsley Weatherhead, "Philip Larkin of England," p. 617.
18. Philip Larkin, "The Savage Seventh," *Spectator*, 20 November 1959, p. 713.
19. *Ibid.*, p. 714.
20. Kuby, *An Uncommon Poet for the Common Man*, p. 22.
21. Weatherhead, "Philip Larkin of England," p. 618.
22. Bedient, *Eight Contemporary Poets*, p. 71.
23. See his recording of *The Whitsun Weddings*.

Chapter Four

1. F. W. Bateson, "Auden's (and Empson's) Heirs," *Essays in Criticism*, 7 (1957), p. 77.
2. Kuby, *An Uncommon Poet for the Common Man*, pp. 127 - 28.
3. Philip Gardner, "The Wintry Drum . . .," p. 92.
4. Kuby, p. 172.
5. "Philip Larkin," in *Poet's Choice*, eds. Paul Engel and Joseph Langland (New York: New Directions Press, 1962), p. 202.
6. See his recording of *The Whitsun Weddings*.
7. *Ibid.*
8. David Timms, *Philip Larkin*, p. 124.
9. *The Crisis in Education*, eds. C. B. Cox and A. E. Dyson (London: Critical Quarterly Society, 1969), p. 133.
10. Timms, *Philip Larkin*, p. 127.
11. Kuby, *An Uncommon Poet for the Common Man*, pp. 160 - 61.

Chapter Five

1. Dan Jacobson, "Profile 3: Philip Larkin," *The New Review*, 1, no. 3 (June 1974), p. 26.
2. Kuby, p. 141.

3. Larkin, "Betjeman en Bloc," p. 20.
4. Edna Langley, "Larkin, Edward Thomas and the Tradition," *Phoenix*, Nos. 11 / 12 (Autumn & Winter, 1973 / 4), p. 84.
5. Kuby, p. 149.
6. Langley, p. 81.
7. Kuby, p. 157.
8. Timms, *Philip Larkin*, p. 62.

Chapter Six

1. Larkin, "Introduction" to *Jill*, 2nd ed., pp. 19 - 20.
2. Philip Larkin, *A Girl in Winter* (London: Faber and Faber), 1947, p. 200. Subsequent quotations are documented in the text.
3. James Gindin, *Postwar British Fiction* (Berkeley: University of California Press, 1962), pp. 99 - 100.
4. Edmund Crispin, "An Oxford Group," *Spectator*, 221 (17 April 1964), p. 525.
5. John Bailey, "Too good for this world," *Times Literary Supplement*, 21 June 1974, p. 653.
6. Philip Larkin, "Wanted: Good Hardy Critic," *Critical Quarterly*, 8 (Summer 1966), p. 179.
7. Philip Larkin, "Mrs. Hardy's Memories," *Critical Quarterly*, 4 (Spring 1962), pp. 75 - 79; [untitled review of Lona Packer's *Christina Rosetti* and her edition of *The Rosetti-MacMillan Letters*], *Listener*, 26 March 1964, p. 526.
8. Philip Larkin, "The War Poet," *The Listener*, 10 October 1963, p. 561.
9. Philip Larkin, "Big Victims: Emily Dickinson and Walter de la Mare," *New Statesman*, 13 March 1970, pp. 367 - 68; [untitled review of Lona Packer's *Christina Rosetti* and her edition of *The Rosetti-Macmillan Letters*.
10. Larkin, "Wanted: Good Hardy Critic," p. 175.
11. Larkin, "The War Poet," p. 562.
12. Philip Larkin, "The Most Victorian Laureate," *New Statesman*, 14 March 1969, p. 364.

Chapter Seven

1. Philip Larkin, "Stevie, good-bye," *Observer*, 23 January 1972, p. 28.
2. David Timms, *Philip Larkin*, pp. 28 - 29.
3. Lolette Kuby, *An Uncommon Poet for the Common Man*, p. 160.
4. Elizabeth Jennings, "The Larkin Tone," *Spectator*, 23 September 1966, p. 386.
5. Kuby, pp. 162 - 63.
6. Timms, p. 30.
7. Kuby, p. 165.

8. In *Poetry in the Making. Catalogue of an Exhibition of Poetry Manuscripts in the British Museum*, ed. Jenny Lewis (London: Turret Books, 1967), pp. 14 - 21.

9. Alan Brownjohn, "The Deep Blue Air," *New Statesman*, 87 (14 June 1975), p. 854.

10. *Ibid.*

Chapter Eight

1. M. L. Rosenthal, "Tuning in on Albion," *The Nation*, 188 (1959), pp. 458 - 59.

2. M. L. Rosenthal, *The New Poets. American and British Poets Since World War II* (New York: Oxford University Press, 1967), p. 234.

3. Colin Falck, "Philip Larkin," in *The Modern Poet*, ed. Ian Hamilton (New York: Horizon Press, 1969), p. 108.

4. Donald Hall, "Poet of Stones and Field," *Nation*, 221 (6 December 1975), p. 600.

5. John Matthias, "Foreword" to *23 Modern Poets* (Chicago: The Swallow Press, 1971), p. xiii.

6. Donald Davie, *Thomas Hardy and British Poetry* (New York: Oxford University Press, 1972), p. 64.

7. John Press, *A Man of Modern English Verse* (London: Oxford University Press, 1969), p. 204.

8. Calvin Bedient, "High Windows," *New York Times Book Review*, 12 January 1975, p. 3.

9. Clive James, "Wolves of Memory," *Encounter*, 42 (June 1975), p. 65.

10. Louis Martz, "Recent Poetry: The Substance of Change," *Yale Review*, 54 (Summer 1965), p. 609.

11. Bedient, "High Windows," p. 14.

12. Kuby, *An Uncommon Poet for the Common Man*, p. 187.

13. Amis made his remarks on a BBC broadcast honoring Larkin on his fiftieth birthday.

14. Calvin Bedient, *Eight Contemporary Poets*, p. 71.

15. Davie, *Thomas Hardy and British Poetry*, p. 69.

16. A remark made on a BBC broadcast; see note number 13.

17. Philip Gardner, "The Wintry Drum . . .," p. 71.

18. Ian Hamilton, "The Whitsun Weddings," *London Magazine*, n.s. 4 (May 1964), p. 71.

19. James K. Robinson, "Terror Lumped and Split: Contemporary British and American Poets," *Southern Review*, n.s. 6 (1970), p. 223.

20. See R.S. Crane, "Questions and Answers in the Teaching of Literary Texts," in *The Idea of the Humanities*, II (Chicago: University of Chicago Press, 1967), pp. 176 - 93.

21. Clive James, p. 66.

22. William Van O'Connor, *The New University Wits* (Carbondale:

Southern Illinois University Press, 1963), p. 29.

   23. Kuby, *An Uncommon Poet for the Common Man*, pp. 13 - 14.

   24. *Ibid.*, pp. 19 - 21.

   25. Irving Howe, *Literary Modernism* (New York: Fawcett Publication, 1967), p. 35.

   26. See William M. Chace, "*Ulysses:* Caritas or Puzzles?" *Novel*, 10, no. 3 (Spring 1977), 265 - 69.

Selected Bibliography

The following represents a complete listing of Larkin's published writings, including the contents of *XX Poems* and the three principal collections of poetry, plus a highly selective listing of books, articles, and reviews of particular value in studying him.

PRIMARY SOURCES

1. Poetry Collections

The North Ship. London: The Fortune Press, 1945. 2nd edition, introduced, and with an additional poem taken from *XX Poems*, by Philip Larkin, London: Faber and Faber, 1966.

XX Poems. Privately printed in a limited edition of 100. Belfast, 1951. Includes the following poems plus those listed under *The Less Deceived* followed by an asterisk: "Wedding-wind"; "Modesties"; "Arrival"; "[Since the majority of me]"; "[Waiting for breakfast, while she brushed her hair]" (later included in the 2nd edition of *The North Ship*); "Two portraits of sex; (1) Oils (2) Etching"; "[Who called love conquering]"; "The dedicated."

The Fantasy Poets. Philip Larkin. Swineford: The Fantasy Press, 1954. (All five of the poems in this pamphlet were republished in *The Less Deceived* and are indicated below by a double-asterisk.)

The Less Deceived. Hessle, Yorkshire: The Marvell Press, 1954. Includes the following poems: "Lines on a Young Lady's Photograph Album";** "Wedding-Wind";* "Coming";* "Reasons for Attendance"; "Dry-Point"* (originally appeared in *XX Poems* as "Etching"); "Next, Please";* "Going";* "Wants";* "Maiden Name"; "Born Yesterday"; "Whatever Happened?";** "No Road";* "Wires";* "Church Going"; "Age"; "Myxomatosis"; "Toads"; "Poetry of Departures"; "Triple Time"; "Spring";* "Deceptions"* (originally titled "The Less Deceived"); "I Remember, I Remember"; "Absences"; "Latest Face";* "If, My Darling";* ** "Skin"; "Arrivals, Departures";** "At Grass."*

The Whitsun Weddings. London: Faber and Faber, 1964. Includes the following poems: "Here"; "Mr. Bleaney"; "Nothing to be Said"; "Love Songs in Age"; "Naturally the Foundation Will Bear Your Expenses"; "Broadcast"; "Faith Healing"; "For Sidney Bechet"; "Home Is So Sad"; "Toads Revisited"; "Water"; "The Whitsun Wed-

dings"; "Self's the Man"; "Take One Home for the Kiddies";
"Days"; "MCMXIV"; "Talking in Bed"; "The Large Cool Store"; "A
Study of Reading Habits"; "As Bad as a Mile"; "Ambulances"; "The
Importance of Elsewhere"; "Sunny Prestatyn"; "First Sight";
"Dockery and Son"; "Ignorance"; "Reference Back"; "Wild Oats";
"Essential Beauty"; "Send No Money"; "Afternoons"; "An Arundel
Tomb."

High Windows. London: Faber and Faber, 1974. Includes the following
poems: "To the Sea"; "Sympathy in White Major"; "The Trees";
"Livings"; "Forget What Did"; "High Windows"; "Friday Night in
the Royal Station Hotel"; "The Old Fools"; "Going, Going"; "The
Card-Players"; "The Building"; "Posterity"; "Dublinesque";
"Homage to a Government"; "This Be the Verse"; "How Distant";
"Sad Steps"; "Solar"; "Annus Mirabilis"; "Vers de Société"; "Show
Saturday"; "Money"; "Cut Grass"; "The Explosion."

2. Uncollected Poems (since 1945)
"Fiction and the Reading Public." *Essays in Criticism*, 4 (January 1954),
86.
"Pigeons." *Departure*, January 1957, p. 2.
"Tops." *Listen*, 2 (Spring 1957), 6.
"Success Story." *Beloit Poetry Journal*, 8 (Winter 1957 - 58), 36.
"Breadfruit." *Critical Quarterly*, 3 (Winter 1961), 309.
"Love." *Critical Quarterly*, 8 (Summer 1966), 173.
[Untitled Couplet] in *The Crisis in Education*, ed. C. B. Cox and A. E.
Dyson. London: Critical Quarterly Society, 1969. p. 133.
"How." *Wave*, Autumn 1970, p. 32.
"Heads in the Women's Ward." *New Humanist*, 1 (May 1972), 17.
"Continuing to Live." in *A Keepsake from the New Library*. A pamphlet
privately printed in a limited edition of 1,000. London, 1973. p. [5].

3. Prose Books
Jill. London: The Fortune Press, 1946. 2nd edition, introduced by Philip
Larkin, London: Faber and Faber, 1964.
A Girl in Winter. London: Faber and Faber, 1947.
All What Jazz. A Record Diary 1961 - 68. London: Faber and Faber, 1970.

4. Uncollected Criticism and Essays
"No More Fever." *Listen*, 2 (Summer 1956), 22 - 26.
"The Writer in His Age: Philip Larkin." *London Magazine*, 4 (May 1957),
46 - 47.
"The Pleasure Principle." *Listen*, 2 (Summer-Autumn 1957), 28 - 32.
"No Fun Any More." *The Manchester Guardian*, 18 November 1958, p. 4.
"Betjeman en Bloc." *Listen*, 3 (Spring 1959), 14 - 22.
"Not the Place's Fault." Umbrella, 1 (Summer 1959), 107 - 12.

"The Savage Seventh." *The Spectator,* 20 November 1959, pp. 713 - 14.

"John Press: *Guy Fawkes Night and other poems.*" *Critical Quarterly,* 1 (Winter 1959), 362 - 63.

"What's Become of Wystan?" *The Spectator,* 15 July 1960, pp. 104 - 105.

"The Blending of Betjeman." *The Spectator,* 2 December 1960, p. 913.

"Context: Philip Larkin." *London Magazine,* 1 (February 1962), 31 - 32.

"Masters' Voices." *New Statesman,* 2 February 1962, pp. 170 - 71.

"Mrs. Hardy's Memories." *Critical Quarterly,* 4 (Spring 1962), 75 - 79.

"The Poetry of William Barnes." *The Listener,* 16 August 1962, p. 257.

"Frivolous and Vulnerable." *New Statesman,* 28 September 1962, p. 416f.

"Absences." In *Poet's Choice,* ed. Paul Engel and Joseph Langland. New York: New Directions Press, 1962. pp. 202 - 203.

"The War Poet." *The Listener,* 10 October 1963, pp. 561 - 62.

"*Christina Rossetti* by Lona Mosk Packer; *The Rossetti-Macmillan Letters.* Edited by Lona Mosk Packer." *Listener,* 26 March 1964, p. 526.

"Wanted: Good Hardy Critic." *Critical Quarterly,* 8 (Summer 1966), 174 - 79.

"Operation Manuscript." In *Poetry in the Making: A Catalogue of an Exhibition of Poetry Manuscripts in the British Museum, April-June, 1967.* ed. Jenny Lewis. London: Turret Books, 1967, pp. 14 - 21.

"Philip Larkin praises the poetry of Thomas Hardy." *Listener,* 25 July 1968, p. 111.

"The Apollo Bit." *New Statesman,* 14 June 1968, p. 798ff.

"The Most Victorian Laureate." *New Statesman,* 14 March 1969, pp. 363 - 64.

"Big Victims: Emily Dickinson and Walter de la Mare." *New Stateman,* 13 March 1970, pp. 367 - 68.

"It could only happen in England." *The Cornhill,* 1969 (Autumn 1971), 21 - 36. Also published as the Introduction to John Betjeman's *Collected Poems,* enlarged edition, compiled by the Earl of Birkenhead. Boston: Houghton Mifflin, 1971.

"Palgrave's Last Anthology: A. E. Housman's Copy." *Review of English Studies,* n.s. 22 (1971), 312 - 16.

"Stevie, good-bye." *Observer,* 23 January 1972, p. 28.

"The Hidden Hardy." *New Statesman,* 2 June 1972, pp. 752 - 53.

"The State of Poetry—A Symposium: Philip Larkin." *The Review,* 29 - 30 (Spring-Summer 1972), 60.

"Worksheets of 'At Grass.'" *Phoenix,* Nos. 11 / 12 (Autumn & Winter, 1973 / 4), 91 - 104.

"The Real Wilfred. Owen's Life and Legends." *Encounter,* 44 (March 1975), 73 - 81.

5. Editions by Larkin

New Poems. ed. Philip Larkin, Louis MacNiece, and Bonamy Dobree. London: Michael Joseph, 1958.

The Oxford Book of Twentieth-Century English Verse. ed. Philip Larkin.
London: Oxford University Press, 1973.

6. Recordings
"Philip Larkin Reads *The Less Deceived.*" Hessle, Yorkshire: Listen
Records, 1958, reissued 1968. The sleeve note of the 1958 release is a
publishing history of *The Less Deceived;* in 1968 it is a short interview
with Larkin on reading his poems.
"Philip Larkin Reads and Comments on *The Whitsun Weddings.*" Hessle,
Yorkshire: Listen Records, 1965.

SECONDARY SOURCES

ALVAREZ, ALFRED. "Poetry of the Fifties in England." *International
Literary Annual No. 1,* ed. John Wain. London: John Calder, 1958, pp. 97 -
107. An early assessment of The Movement and Larkin's place in it.
ANON. "Four Young Poets—I: Philip Larkin." *Times Educational Supple-
ment,* 13 July 1956, p. 933. An early interview with Larkin, offering
some interesting biographical information.
———. "In the Movement." *Spectator,* 193 (1 October 1954), 399 - 400.
The first public recognition and discussion of The Movement; a
significant article.
BALL, PATRICIA. "The Photographic Art." *Review of English Literature,* 3
(April 1962), 50 - 58. Relates The Movement to the English Realistic
tradition; argues that The Movement takes Realism one step further in
terms of honesty.
BATESON, F. W. "Auden's (and Empson's) Heirs." *Essays in Criticism,* 7
(1957), 76 - 80. A review of *The Less Deceived* and Davie's *Brides of
Reason;* relates The Movement to the Augustans.
BEDIENT, CALVIN. *Eight Contemporary Poets.* London: Oxford University
Press, 1974, pp. 69 - 94. A very thoughtful tracing of Larkin's development as a poet, the special technical qualities of his verse, the moral
qualities of his outlook, and his relationship to his outstanding contemporaries. A valuable discussion.
———. "High Windows." *New York Times Book Review,* 12 January 1975,
pp. 3f. An interesting review of Larkin's latest collection, relating it to
his earlier writings and to contemporary poetry in general.
BERGONZI, BERNARD. "After 'The Movement,' " *The Listener,* 66 (1961),
284 - 85. Describes concisely the common origins, influences, and
techniques of Movement writers.
BLUM, MARGARET. "Larkin's Dry-Point." *Explicator,* 32 (February 1974),
48. Close analysis of the diction in this one poem.
CHAMBERS, HARRY. "Some Light Views of a Serious Poem: a footnote to the
misreading of Philip Larkin's 'Naturally the Foundation Will Bear
Your Expenses.' " *Phoenix,* 11 / 12 (Autumn & Winter,
1973 / 4—Philip Larkin Issue), 110 - 14. Examines the distance

between Larkin and his speaker by comparing the poem to others by Owen and Tennyson.

CONQUEST, ROBERT. "Introduction" to *New Lines*. London: Macmillan & Co., 1956, pp. xi - xviii. Generally regarded as the Movement manifesto; defines the stance associated with *The Movement*.

COX, C. B. "Philip Larkin." *Critical Quarterly*, 1 (Spring 1959), 14 - 17. An early attempt to distinguish Larkin from other Movement writers.

DAVIE, DONALD. "Landscapes of Larkin," in *Thomas Hardy and British Poetry*. New York: Oxford University Press, 1972, pp. 63 - 82. Because Davie sees Hardy as the most important influence on twentieth-century British verse, he finds Larkin an important contemporary writer; draws interesting connections, particularly political ones, between Larkin and Hardy.

DODSWORTH, MARTIN. "The Climate of Pain in Recent Poetry." *London Magazine*, n.s. 4 (November 1964), 86 - 95. An appreciative discussion of poems in *The Whitsun Weddings*.

FALCK, COLIN. "Philip Larkin," in *The Modern Poet*. ed. Ian Hamilton. New York: Horizon Press, 1969, pp. 101 - 10. Criticizes Larkin's brand of humanism.

FIELDLER, LESLIE A.. "Class War in British Literature." *Esquire*, 49 (April 1958), 79 - 81. A very provocative account of The Angry Young men, whom Fieldler equates with The Movement. Particularly keen on drawing out political implications of the literary revolt of the 1950s in Britain.

FRASER, G. S. *Vision and Rhetoric: Studies in Modern Poetry*. London: Faber and Faber, 1959. Essays on various aspects and figures of modern poetry, including comments on Larkin; useful for determining the immediate literary background out of which Larkin's poems emerged.

GARDNER, PHILIP. "The Wintry Drum: The Poetry of Philip Larkin." *Dalhousie Review*, 48 (Spring 1968), 88 - 99. A general discussion of Larkin's attitudes; particularly useful account of differences between *The Less Deceived* and *The Whitsun Weddings*.

GINDIN, JAMES. *Postwar British Fiction*. Berkeley: University of California Press, 1963, pp. 87 - 108. Attempts to relate *Jill* to the working-class-hero phenomenon in British fiction in the 1950s.

GRUBB, FREDERICK. "Dragons." *Phoenix*, 11 / 12 (Autumn & Winter, 1973 / 4), 119 - 36. Examines Larkin's handling of death in a number of recent poems, as well as the topicality of his recent writing.

_____. "No One Actually Starves," in *A Vision of Reality: A Study of Liberalism in Twentieth-Century Verse*. London: Chatto and Windus, 1965, pp. 226 - 41. Examines Larkin's writing in the context of The Movement and the British Welfare State.

HARTLEY, GEORGE. "No Right of Entry." *Phoenix*, 11 / 12 (Autumn & Winter, 1973 / 4), 105 - 109. An analysis of "Dry-Point."

HILL, FRANCIS. "A Sharp-Edged View." *Times Educational Supplement*, 19 May 1972, p. 19. An interview with Larkin.

HOLLOWAY, JOHN. "The Literary Scene," in *The Modern Age* (Vol. 7 of *The Pelican Guide to English Literature*). ed. Boris Ford. Baltimore: Penguin Books, 1961.

HORDER, JOHN. "Poet on the 8.15." *Manchester Guardian*, 20 May 1965, p. 9. An interview with Larkin.

JACOBSON, DAN. "Profile 3: Philip Larkin." *The New Review*, 1, no. 3 (June 1974), 25 - 28. A very provocative account of distinctive elements in Larkin's writing and their relationship to English moral and literary traditions.

JAMES. CLIVE. "Wolves of Memory." *Encounter*, 42 (June 1975), 65 - 71. A review of *High Windows* which agressively defends Larkin against his critics.

JOHNSON, JUDITH ANNE. "The Development of Philip Larkin's Poetry." Unpub. M.A. thesis, North Dakota State University of Agriculture and Applied Science, Fargo, 1965. Includes some letters from Larkin to the author concerning his writing.

JONES, ALUN R. "The Poetry of Philip Larkin: A Note on Translantic Culture." *Western Humanities Review*, 16 (Spring 1962), 143 - 52. An attempt to explain the peculiarily postwar British qualities of Larkin's writing.

KUBY, LOLETTE. *An Uncommon Poet for the Common Man. A Study of Philip Larkin's Poetry*. The Hague: Mouton, 1974. The best extended discussion of Larkin's writing published to date; especially impressive on the attitudes and assumptions in his poetry, the relationship of his poetry to that of earlier and contemporary poets, and the stylistic properties of his writing. Excellent analyses of a number of his poems.

LANGLEY, EDNA. "Larkin, Edward Thomas and the Tradition." *Phoenix*, 11 / 12 (Autumn & Winter, 1973 / 4), 63 - 89. A sensitive, detailed examination of Larkin's concerns and style in comparison with those of Thomas; contains many perceptive observations about the peculiarities of each poet's style.

LOWELL, ROBERT. "Digression on Larkin's Anthology." *Encounter*, 40 (May 1973), 66 - 68. Favorable criticism.

LUCIE-SMITH, EDWARD. "Between Suicide and Revolution: The Poet as Role Player." *Saturday Review*, 19 April 1975, pp. 14 - 18.

NAREMORE, JAMES. "Philip Larkin's 'Lost World'." *Contemporary Literature*, 15 (Summer 1974), 331 - 43. Interestingly contends that, rather than rejecting romanticism in favor of the empirical, Larkin in his mature verse has merely refined his youthful romanticism.

OAKES, PHILIP. "The Unsung Gold Medallist." *Sunday Times Magazine*, 27 March 1966, pp. 63 - 65. Combination of interview and personal portrait; contains many interesting biographical details.

O'CONNOR, WILLIAM VAN. *The New University Wits (and the End of Modernism)*. Carbondale: Southern Illinois University Press, 1963. A series of essays on various figures associated with The Movement; while one of the essays ("PHILIP LARKIN: The Quiet Poem," pp. 16 - 29) concentrates on Larkin, remarks about him and remarks about others which relate to him appear throughout the book. Relates Larkin's novels to his poetry.

OLIVER, DOUGLAS. "Poet Who Captures the Music of Daily Life." *Coventry Evening Telegraph,* 6 October 1972, p. 30. An appreciative portrait of Larkin and his poetic outlook.

PARKINSON, R. N. " 'To Keep Our Metaphysics Warm': A Study of 'Church Going' by Philip Larkin." *Critical Survey,* 5 (Winter 1971), 224 - 33. A detailed analysis.

PESCHMANN, HERMANN. "Philip Larkin: Laureate of the Common Man." *English,* 24 (1975), 49 - 58. A survey of Larkin's development and achievement in verse.

PRESS, JOHN. "The Movement and Poets of the 1950s," in *A Map of Modern English Verse.* London: Oxford University Press, 1969. pp. 251 - 70. A useful summary of The Movement.

PRITCHARD, WILLIAM H. "Larkin Lives." *Hudson Review,* 28 (1975 - 76), 302 - 08. Chides Larkin's defenders for being overly apologetic of their subject.

RODWAY, ALLAN. "A Note on Contemporary English Poetry." *Texas Quarterly,* 4, no. 3 (Autumn 1961), 66 - 72. A survey of the origins of Movement poetry.

ROSENTHAL, M. L. *The New Poets. American and British Poets Since World War II.* New York: Oxford University Press, 1967. A useful account of developments in postwar poetry; sharply critical of Movement poetry, and of Larkin in particular.

————. "Tuning in on Albion." *Nation,* 188 (1959), 458 - 59. A review of *The Less Deceived;* highly critical.

SCHUPHAM, PETER. "A Caucus Race." *Phoenix,* 11 / 12 (Autumn & Winter, 1973 / 4), 173 - 82. A critical review of Larkin's *Oxford Book of Twentieth-Century English Verse.*

SPENDER, STEPHEN. *The Struggle of the Modern.* Berkeley: University of California Press, 1963. An excellent history and analysis of Modernism which places many nonmoderns, including Larkin, in a Modernistic perspective.

STOCK, NOEL. "Lowell and Larkin. *Poetry Australia,* 54 (1975) 74 - 79. Judges Larkin the superior.

THWAITE, ANTHONY. "Larkin, Philip." *Contemporary Poets of the English Language,* ed. Rosalie Murphy. Chicago and London: St. James Press, 1970, pp. 628 - 30. Contains essential biographical and publishing data.

————. "Larkin's Recent Uncollected Poems." *Phoenix,* 11 / 12 (Autumn & Winter, 1973 / 4), 59 - 61. Brief comments by a critic sensitive to what Larkin is about.

————. "The Poetry of Philip Larkin." in *The Survival of Poetry: A*

Contemporary Survey, ed. Martin Dodsworth. London: Faber and Faber, 1970, pp. 37 - 55. A key essay discussing the technical features of Larkins poetry, his relationship to The Movement, and his development.

TIMMS, DAVID. " 'Church Going' Revisited: 'The Building' and the Notion of Development in Larkin's Poetry." *Phoenix*, 11 / 12 (Autumn & Winter, 1973 / 4), 13 - 26. Measures his development by comparing his recent treatment of institutions with his earlier treatments. Interesting.

———. *Philip Larkin*. New York: Barnes and Noble, 1973. The first published book on Larkin. Contains much useful information; especially helpful for seeing Larkin's poems in their biographical and British contexts.

WALSH, CHAD. "The Postwar Revolt in England Against Modern Poets." *Bucknell Review*, 13 (December 1965), 97 - 105. A very thoughtful reflection on the nature and implications of The Movement.

WATSON, J. R. "The Other Larkin." *Critical Quarterly*, 17 (1975), 347 - 60. Praises the profundity of many Larkin poems.

WEATHERHEAD, A. KINGSLEY. "Philip Larkin of England." *ELH*, 38 (December 1971), 616 - 30. A perceptive analysis of Larkin's characteristic attitudes and techniques, their relationship to larger developments in British poetry, and changes in Larkin's writing since *The North Ship*.

WEISS, THEDORE. "The Flight of Modernisn and Philip Larkin's Antidote." *American Poetry Review*, 6, no. 1 (Jan. / Feb., 1977), 39 - 41. Defends modernism.

Index

(The works of Larkin are listed under his name)